"To José Vadi, one of our great poets of the overlooked and ig-nored, it's not just a skateboard. It's a medium for dreaming, for chasing down histories of public space and private rebellion, for measuring ourselves against the wide-open visions of youth. *Chipped* is a treasure."   —Hua Hsu, winner of the 2023
Pulitzer Prize for *Stay True*

"Vadi conjures California's charms through descriptions of invit-ingly empty parking lots, curbs perfectly waxed for skating, per-ilously designed intersections and the shimmering temptation of stairways and railings . . . Skateboarding as Vadi understands it is an act of defiance, a story that isn't usually written. Part of what makes his documenting it powerful is the proof that a life like this is possible . . . *Chipped* bears the marks of everything Vadi learned on his board. His prose is often vivid and propul-sive . . . In skating, Vadi found 'a compass, a lens, a portal to joy only found by trying.' *Chipped* offers the same even to those of us who have never stepped onto a board."

—Zan Romanoff, *Los Angeles Times*

"Oakland and San Francisco loom large in José Vadi's skateboard-ing memoir-in-essays . . . Together, these pieces examine how skateboarding has influenced culture, power and art."

—Hannah Bae, *San Francisco Chronicle*

"If his debut essay collection, *Inter State*, offered a series of love letters to California, *Chipped* is an extended mash note to the rich subculture of the board."   —Emily St. Martin, *Alta*

"José Vadi's essay collection shines in its quiet power; his writing and description builds to an impressive crescendo, or oftentimes, builds to a crescendo before settling down to a profound but never facile revelation. *Chipped* is made up of ten essays that shine in their individuality and as a whole alchemize into a bird's-eye view of the art of skateboarding and its place in a creative life and in a contemporary society that doesn't always value the contemplative life."
                                        —Pete Riehl, *The Chills at Will Podcast*

"Pensive . . . The rhapsodic prose shines, and Vadi's passion will hold the attention even of readers who know little about the sport. It's a ride well worth taking."
                                        —*Publishers Weekly* (starred review)

"A luminous reflection on the many ways that skateboarding changes the way we see the world from one of our most attentive pairs of eyes and ears."   —Ted Barrow, writer, art historian,
                                                      and skateboarder

"*Chipped* is a paean to a time before subcultures could be found with the click of a button. In this chronicle of the joyful, humbling, lifelong work of discovery, José Vadi shows how skateboarding can redraw the map of a city, a life, a world."
                                        —Nina Renata Aron, author of *Good Morning,*
                                                      Destroyer of Men's Souls

"Continue the line that runs from Sun Ra to contemporary skateboarding and you'll arrive at the brilliant, searching essays of José Vadi. *Chipped* is a masterpiece of both the form and his subject."
                                        —Kyle Beachy, author of *The Most Fun Thing*

"In *Inter State: Essays on California* José Vadi provides us with a portrait of California's past, present, and future, often through family and personal history and sometimes on a skateboard. Now, with *Chipped*, Vadi is firmly embedded in skateboarding's ecosystem: the circulation of culture through VHS tapes, zines, and magazines, the well-documented but nonetheless clandestine history of skate spots, the transgressive use of public space, and the often painful integration of one's body with the built environment. More than this, *Chipped* reminds us all—skaters and non-skaters—that failure is inevitable and that the ultimate tragedy is to not try, to not push forward. *Chipped* will establish Vadi as an essential voice in California letters." —Romeo Guzmán, assistant professor at Claremont Graduate University and coeditor of *East of East: The Making of Greater El Monte*

"A skateboard is a simple plaything from which a vibrant global culture emerged. With *Chipped*, José Vadi takes us under the hood of its animating force, deftly weaving the personal with the world to show us how all the infinitely beautiful and complicated things that make us human coalesce to breathe life into this toy. A piece of wood with wheels that can, if you let it, take you everywhere and show you everything." —Cole Nowicki, author of *Right, Down + Circle* and *Laser Quit Smoking Massage*

"In these vibrant texts, José Vadi shows how skateboarding is not a sport but an attitude, a culture, a way of thinking. A compelling collection of insights, musings, and observations." —Iain Borden, author of *Skateboarding and the City: A Complete History*

"Skateboarders young and old-school will see themselves in Vadi's journey captured in this collection of essays by an optimistic, fresh, and insightful voice."   *—Booklist*

"The essays are poetic, compassionate, and vulnerable, drawing rewardingly original connections among a host of seemingly disparate topics . . . Vadi clearly takes great pleasure in the vocabulary and syntax of skateboarding; at times, this pleasure feels contagious, even for non-skaters. . . [A] largely illuminating collection about skateboarding, race, and relationships."

—Kirkus Reviews

CHIPPED

ALSO BY JOSÉ VADI

Inter State: Essays from California

CHIPPED

WRITING FROM A

SKATEBOARDER'S LENS

JOSÉ VADI

SOFT SKULL

NEW YORK

Chipped

This is a work of nonfiction. However, some names and identifying details of individuals have been changed to protect their privacy, correspondence has been shortened for clarity, and dialogue has been reconstructed from memory.

Copyright © 2024 by José Vadi

All rights reserved under domestic and international copyright. Outside of fair use (such as quoting within a book review), no part of this publication may be reproduced, stored in a retrieval system, or transmitted in any form or by any means, electronic, mechanical, photocopying, recording, or otherwise, without the written permission of the publisher. For permissions, please contact the publisher.

First Soft Skull edition: 2024
First paperback edition: 2025

Image on pages 146–47 courtesy of Ed Templeton and *Transworld Skateboarding.*

The Library of Congress has cataloged the hardcover edition as follows:
Names: Vadi, José, author.
Title: Chipped : writing from a skateboarder's lens / José Vadi.
Description: First Soft Skull edition. | New York : Soft Skull, [2024]
Identifiers: LCCN 2023041070 | ISBN 9781593767556 (hardcover) | ISBN 9781593767563 (ebook)
Subjects: LCSH: Vadi, José. | Skateboarding—Social aspects. | Skateboarders—California—Biography.
Classification: LCC GV859.8 .V34 2024 | DDC 796.22092 B—dc23/eng/20231023
LC record available at https://lccn.loc.gov/2023041070

Paperback ISBN: 978-1-59376-797-6

Cover design by www.houseofthought.io
Cover photograph courtesy of the author
Book design by Laura Berry

Published by Soft Skull Press
New York, NY
www.softskull.com

Printed in the United States of America

10 9 8 7 6 5 4 3 2 1

CONTENTS

INTRODUCTION

I started skateboarding in 1996, around the start of what some would call the industry's creative and economic boom, and even as a newcomer, I could feel it: magazines were getting thicker with advertisements; independent skate-shoe companies were creating bolder, more innovative designs; and there was even a rumor Tony Hawk was getting a video game. The technological standard for independently produced skate videos started changing, going from Hi8 tape cameras in the mid-1990s to digital, high-definition captures with fish-eye lenses by the early 2000s. Skateboarding's history is nascent and granular, with some trends spanning just months rather than years, but entering a new scene at one of its cultural heights made me believe everything in skateboarding was important. Every photo, soundtrack, board graphic, even the way a skater tied their shoelaces—it was vital to understand and model everything. I fell in love with not only skateboarding in 1996 but the ability to obsess. To connect with other skaters in different environments, realizing myself now outside, on four wheels, navigating a world remade by the joy moving me forward.

This is not a chronicle of my greatest tricks landed on a

board or of skateboarding days gone by. *Chipped* is my articulation of how skateboarding gave me a new lens to see my world and myself differently.

Today, when I meet a skater in a non-skateboarding setting, there's an immediate recognition of the lens we share: a lens that understands that passions can be criminalized, that the term *public space* is asterisked, and that space is as much a construct as time. As skaters we observe the potential of a ledge with specs that also apply to an awareness of public space, noting that the knobs, clamps, and skate-stoppers installed on ledges to prevent them from being skated resemble those larger rocks conveniently placed in areas where the unhoused may seek refuge. We will skate either the sketchy neighborhood or the ritzy mansion to avoid the plague of inaction and missed opportunities. From the physical to the figurative, everything will break; the heroism is in the act, not in medals. Through experience and through sharing space during skate sessions, we begin to understand those unspoken rules and the etiquette skaters organically define. We know the stubbornness of trying tricks all day as well as the seeming futility in attempting to describe a hobby where we roll our ankles and destroy our knees and bruise our elbows and ribs every weekend. There's a recognition that this lens propels and catalyzes, alters actions as much as perceptions, and changes lives, sometimes for the worse. For mind to direct body toward action is a remarkable feat, I realize, particularly the older we get, and skateboarding fortifies the desire inside of us to go outside and try, if we're lucky.

I started writing what would become *Chipped* while my publisher and I were sending out advance reader copies of my first book, *Inter State: Essays from California*. Detailing my familial and personal connections to California, *Inter State* was written in one world, Oakland, and the finished books arrived in another, Sacramento. *Inter State* is full of movement—road trips, pedestrian jaunts across neighborhoods, and every form of public transportation available—but a lot of it was crafted in a sedentary state in a nook of my apartment at the height of the pandemic.

My release during this time was skateboarding, learning how to slappy curbs and staying literally connected to the streets of Oakland as a testament to the skate spots, neighborhoods, and cities I took for granted, never thinking I'd leave. Despite this, I'd come home to a sense of sustained claustrophobia. As the pandemic worsened throughout 2020, I realized I might be in this sedentary state for much longer than expected.

Inter State was an exercise in writing from a specific place at a specific moment in that place, but many of the routine-driven Bay Area movements detailed in that book were increasingly prohibited by the pandemic. It's hard to replicate running after a critical bus connection by walking around an empty Safeway parking lot five times, avoiding people, and feeling proud to be outside, moving once again. From a state of inertia I feared that I was writing myself out of my Bay Area existence by making *Inter State*, which became an elegiac process to memorialize my existence within the space I'd called home for roughly two decades.

Skateboarding can be many things in a person's life throughout their years of experience, and for me, it became a compatriot, accompanying me through these changing times, from the Bay Area to Sacramento. Like I'd feared writing myself out of a place, I feared that writing about skateboarding might create a similar distance, or an alienation, which is why I didn't write about the act, toy, or culture for years, despite the fact that skate references made natural cameos in my writing. I realized I was already writing with a skateboarder's lens even though skateboarding wasn't a central focus of my work.

If *Inter State* was a monument to the ancestors who led me to California, *Chipped* is written for the friends—close and first-name-only relationships—with whom I grew up skating, those who shared this obsession and by proxy fueled my pursuit of the creative things that skateboarding inspired, like writing.

The cover of this book is a 35 mm photo I took some time in the late 1990s of my friend AJ. His elbows are red from slamming, trying to do a trick down a picnic table set down a three-stair at a local elementary school. When I think about growing up skating, I think about this photo. I was trying to frame my favorite skater, the one who made even bailing a trick seem elegant, dramatic the way he'd evade harsher slams. And though this time AJ wasn't so lucky—his arms red from stubborn falls—it wasn't for lack of trying; trying is what skateboarding is all about as a kid, trying to do anything but rot inside.

AJ is no longer on this earth, and this photo was one of many that helped me realize we were documenting attempts and discovering failures. The fuckups and the accomplishments of skateboarding, held in equal weight and measure across those film negatives, were our initial steps toward discovering ourselves and our personalities. *Chipped* recalls those improvised communities that close friends and strangers alike can create and the alchemy of these moments felt both on and off the board.

That's what I love about the culture of skateboarding and its many strands of music, identity, race, art, architecture, cities, dance, design, education, gender, mutual aid, and urban planning—everything it has the potential to represent. If we talk about it.

It's this lens I'm using to articulate this work and the many dimensions in which skateboarding has impacted, and continues to impact, my life, now in Sacramento, California.

CHIPPED

1.

CHIPPED

I skated my favorite deck so long that its final, abused form
was a mangled rocket ship. All deformed, bruised nose and
short, flattened tail. I rode that baby-blue board off sets of
stairs and loading docks for months, slid it across curbs and
benches, threw it in the bushes to enter places that didn't allow
skateboards, returning to find it lying there, undisturbed and
unwanted by those unfamiliar with its magic potential.

It was a shop board sold by my local Utility Board Shop,
the store's logo just above the four drill marks, two by two,
for the back truck's baseplate and the hardware holding it
together. The *l* in *Utility* was given an Olympic torch treatment. It was probably skinny as hell for the era and my age,
less than eight inches wide and perfect for a thirteen-year-old.
Shop boards were cheaper than pro boards and slightly more
expensive than factory blanks, since they were dipped in a
coat of paint and maybe had the shop's logo slapped on somewhere painfully obvious. Pro-model boards paid the skater
a certain amount per sale, while the artists went from being
paid hourly rates in the early 1990s to flat rates by the decade's
end. The inks, the laminate, the wood, the shipping, the

manufacturing, the storage—all of that is what those prices gauge for.

Growing up, I consistently rode shop boards because of their price point. Big-footed, lanky, and tall, I hit puberty at the same time as I developed my fervent appreciation for skateboarding, with more and more boards snapping upon impact. The Girl Skateboards' Guy Mariano pro board with the Italian flag? Snapped trying a kickflip down the five-stair at La Verne's municipal water treatment building. The Adrian Lopez pro-model Zero Skateboards deck with the horseman drawing? Snapped on a ledge trick one week into ownership, before I could even chip the board by accident.

But it was this sky-blue shop board that felt so proper, so intrinsic to my skateboarding at the time, that upgrading to a new board and discarding whatever opportunities the shop board still held seemed akin to self-harm. We had learned how to coexist for this many weeks, months, after all—why not see how long it would last?

Fear of change is both superstition and microcosm, an approach to the tools of our joy that says something about what those joyful dimensions really look and feel like. Skaters approach each trick attempt with muscle memory and a confidence affected by cracks in the sidewalk, sirens on the streets, and fear. With every board, we create a ledger of everything learned and experienced upon it: The more centered the middle board marks, the better the boardslides. Front truck hangers jaggedly destroyed in a forty-five-degree pattern showcase attempted crooked grinds. I liked writing random crap on my stickers as they got shredded, or at my most dreamy scrawling CARPE DIEM in Wite-Out on the grip tape just above the back truck along the side. As if I would forget to seize the day at age twelve, thirteen, and beyond. Let alone for something as addictive as skateboarding.

Now I consider why I didn't get a better used deck or save for a clean, new version of a toy I used every day. A toy that can travel across time and space, measure how fast my body can adjust to a crack before the takeoff point at the top of some stairs, or muscle through a grind along a worn, chewed, concrete ledge.

So much of discovering actual, core skateboarding is literally acquiring its component parts. Before I could afford skate shops, I found most of my first pairs of trucks, sets of wheels, and even shoes through friends. Identifying skaters by their gear allowed conversations about skating to happen, with skate fashions a Bat-Signal as much as a shield against mainstream society. We would also identify each other by our bruises and scabs on the elbows that indicated regular or goofy footed. The torn sneakers. The arm casts and finger splints or, in my case years later, crutches from a sprained knee. They'd hand down or resell to me their Thunder trucks, or their first-model éS Eric Koston pro-model shoes; the toes chewed away on the side of my weaker lead foot afforded the shoes a second life on a skater with a different stance.

Chipping a board is a natural part of skating. A chip is a small piece of board that breaks off around the nose or tail from the wear and tear of skateboarding. Novice or pro, skaters will ride chipped boards, but when you're a kid, chipping your board is kind of a rite of passage. Without disposable income, kids ride boards until they nearly disintegrate, the grip tape all mashed up and mangled along the edges where wood used to be.

Filling in the chips keeps the board going as long as possible. It's a symbol of the stubborn dedication to a deck and to a toy as skaters and as adults, whose bodies will also reach their inevitable end. But the toy evolves beyond a fad and becomes something more—a compass, a lens, a portal to joy only found by trying and failing along the way. The irony is the older I get, the more I empathize with those chipped boards I had as a kid: hiding marks and blemishes while maintaining the semblance of a skater as an adult, not wanting to be discarded, wanting to still be seen as useful, functional, and skating, bruised and chipped, for as long as possible.

2.

SICK BOY

It felt necessary to go outside and skate after *Thrasher* magazine's Jake Phelps died in March 2019. Not that he would've given a damn what I did, the now-departed enfant terrible of skateboarding, whose knowledge of the culture's history was only outmatched by his ability to piss people off.

I decided that morning to skate an older cruiser board across town, something that by name and definition should make for a mellow ride. The board was a Krooked Zig Zagger with a zoomed-in photo of a slice of supreme pizza for a bottom graphic. It had a shaped, pointed nose, a flat shovel of a tail, and soft orange Spitfire cruiser wheels with a faded mock Zig-Zag rolling papers graphic. The board was maybe seven years old at that point, and I had changed out the bearings every so often and used the board mainly as transportation from BART to my apartment in Adams Point. When I had moved in with my girlfriend in Rockridge, I still skated to BART but now far from regularly.

It had been months since my last proper session. It's hard as a skater to find one's place within skateboarding's culture at any point in time, let alone at times when work, commutes, and other creative outlets occupy more of the front of mind. Days and weeks turned into months without skateboarding. Doubt crept in. Then fear. Then malaise.

Still, I left the house and went skating—already a win. Off I went down Broadway and toward the bike lanes connecting Rockridge with neighboring Temescal, from Fifty-First to Fortieth Streets, skating the distance of two BART stops. It was a trip feeling the sensory overload again, responding to every crack, car, stop sign, smell, and sound around me.

I was a month into unemployment after a tech layoff, and a beer felt in order. The corner bar was open and ready for my stupidity. George Kaye's has been around since just after Prohibition and is probably the cleanest of the older bars in Oakland. The neon lights outside read GEO KAYE'S, but the original owner was indeed George. Not the kind of place to know or care what Yelp is. Local-ball-game-on-the-tube-TV-aloft-in-a-corner kind of bar, where the finest technology is a CD jukebox and maybe a digital antenna forced upon the owners during the broadband switch decades ago.

I sat on the short side of the L-shaped bar, facing the Giants spring training game. I started a tab. One Red Stripe turned into two. I thought about Phelps, how I'd miss the stories he shared with the public and how the magazine would be assuredly fine. In the High Speed Productions portfolio, *Thrasher* is the vanguard—and the vanguard for print and digital skateboard media worldwide. I recalled to myself the stories about Phelps: getting hit by an SF MUNI bus and surviving; always running his well-informed foul mouth; banning pro skaters from *Thrasher*; almost dying in a van full of skaters in South Africa after the van's brakes gave out; sitting in another van full of skaters in the mid-1990s when gunshots were fired at it and struck Real Skateboards rider Coco Santiago, injuring him permanently.

And then I realized I didn't have my wallet. I'd put my license and credit card between my phone and its protective case, not planning to be here, an infamously cash-only bar. The ATM across the street surprisingly wouldn't accept my credit card. I was stuck. The bartender was an older gentleman with combed-back hair and a demeanor that said "veteran of foreign service." I feared he thought I was going to offer my board as collateral, as probably other skaters and punks before me had tried to do, but who am I kidding. He could tell I was good for it. I called my girlfriend and asked her to drive down with cash and spot her jobless, walletless guy some bread in his tight squeeze, or whatever imagined and smooth *White Heat* cutting-room-floor line I didn't use on my girlfriend or the bartender. I tipped well and left. I was rusty not only on a board but on a barstool as well, apparently. She asked if I needed a ride back to our apartment, knowing something I didn't, and I said no, skating off to the nearby high school and skate spot, Oak Tech.

Oakland Technical High School's exterior is all regal columns and half-circle stair stages, a giant palace of an exterior with a traditional high school, including its football field, hiding inside.

It's a spot with historic street skating significance after being featured in 1988's *Sick Boys*. Produced and filmed by

Mack Dawg, the VHS was limited to only one thousand copies worldwide but became an underground classic, showcasing the future legends of San Francisco street skateboarding, notably Mickey Reyes, Jim Thiebaud, Tommy Guerrero, and Oakland's Ron Allen. Many of the skaters featured in the video became owners of companies that are still relevant in the skate industry today, including Deluxe Distribution's roster that broke from the big brands of the 1980s and early '90s.

Shot entirely on Super 8 film and rereleased on DVD in 2008, *Sick Boys* was "free from outside control or industry support," as described by Mack Dawg Productions. In an interview for the blog *The Chrome Ball Incident,* Allen described filming with Dawg as "having a camera on a broomstick. He'd always tell us to go as fast as we wanted because he was confident that he could keep up with us. You'd be skating and look down and here's this little camera floating around." Scenes of Natas Kaupas going up the concrete bank and popping an ollie over trash cans at Oak Tech were ingrained in my mind after I caught up to *Sick Boys* as a skater in the late 1990s.

At the spot, all I could think was that I should go fast, push into the smaller side of the bank, and try to get enough speed to hit the larger part of the concrete bank where Kaupas skated years ago. I ran and jumped on my board, still getting used to the feel of this beat-up cruiser. Overcompensating with my speed, pushing slightly uphill, I approached the bank and suddenly changed my mind. I couldn't decide whether to ollie into the bank or kick out and bail, but I was going too fast to do anything logical, so I tried both—impossible—leading to a chaotic tumble onto chewed-up asphalt. My wheels, already a softer urethane, were more worn than I had thought. My board flew one way and my body another. Landing, I planted my left leg down like a mast raising a white sail of defeat, and I heard a click come screaming from my left knee. All this before my body hit the ground and rolled a couple times, gaining knee and arm scrapes, before I came to a stop, shook.

I remember accidentally staring at the sun, exacerbating my absolute confusion at what had just happened. Most of my life has been spent mumbling across dinner tables and having other unamplified interactions. But I yelled that day. A new voice, previously unknown to my ears and lungs. I'm an idiot, a fool, a dummy, arrogant for not respecting the discipline required to skate . . . anything. What did Phelps say? Something about skateboarding owing you nothing but wheel bite in the rain?

I got up quickly, flexing and bending my knee to confirm it wasn't broken. Every terrible thought was running through my mind: It's my left knee, the already-bad knee, the one I didn't stretch much today or in the dormant weeks preceding this session. I walked around deliriously and rested my hand against one of the concrete pillars supporting the solar car shelters above, all of which didn't exist in the time of *Sick Boys*. I tried to keep moving, but the swelling crept in, announcing how fucked I'd be for . . . weeks? Months?

You okay?

I looked over toward a two-seater pickup truck and saw a dude looking at me, appropriately, like I was an idiot. I don't know, I replied honestly. We did the diagnostic talk about whether I had heard a pop, could bend my knee, needed a ride somewhere. I took him up on that offer, using my board as a cane to walk in his direction.

He introduced himself, explained he was there because he ran the school's theater department, the truck hauling the latest production's set props and odds and ends. I told him about participating in such choral theatrical activities for most of my life, an hour a day from fifth grade through high school graduation, and how it even took me out of state sometimes, and I wondered if he could smell the beers on my breath or see the tree rings in my gray hairs, insecurities all the same. Appreciate this solid and figure it out, I thought. The pain made me delirious enough to pour out my familiarity with Rodgers and Hammerstein's oeuvre as he made a left from the school up Broadway, my knee spasming its way to the top of my mind.

I texted my girlfriend, again, and told her to meet me, again. This time at the 76 station, the one on Broadway by the California College of the Arts. I needed ice and they had it. They were my local gasoline-selling bodega, with a mechanic shop for international cars *only* next door. I told my chariot driver to head that way, and he assured me I could get a ride all the way home but I said ice was the priority. Not that I knew shit about this situation. I was holding everything together in this house of cards I was building on myself—my ability to skate, drink, see skate spots, enjoy theatrical interactions with dudes literally producing theater, nuture my potential marriage—and hoping things got better.

I hobbled, sweating, into the store for ice, paid, and quickly sat down on the curb outside the store. I propped my foot on my board, sideways on its axles and elevated just enough, and surrounded the interior of my left knee cap with ice bags. It wouldn't stop stinging, throbbing with waves of pain. I bent it every so often, knowing I was setting myself up to go stiff, but nothing mattered then. I just felt terrible and probably looked ridiculous when my girlfriend pulled up, again, not needing to ask, What happened?

Did I mention I had just been laid off and had lost my health insurance? All the potential costs were adding up in my mind, not to mention the realization of what'd I'd put my girlfriend through on this lovely afternoon. I swallowed Advil upon arrival at the apartment, debating whether my neighbors downstairs could hear how hurt I was by the sound of my lumbering gait. I could barely bend my leg. My knee was stiffening too quickly. I asked my friend, a doctor, to come over and check out the knee, and they didn't notice any structural damage. Bone bruise was the diagnosis. I sat in my kitchen nook for a month, staring out the kitchen window from Rockridge toward the city and the Bay Bridge.

I spent weeks apologizing to my girlfriend, myself, my doctor friend. I look back at photos from those weeks and see nothing but a giant blue ice pack sharing space with my cat on my leg. Lots of photos taken from a chair, inside. It was all a reminder of how skateboarding is a discipline, a practice, a ritual. Though some people can step off a board and jump back on without interruption, creating magic upon re-arrival, for most of us it's scratching off rust, feeling humbled by the difference between what our mind sees and what our body feels when we step onto our boards, let alone step outside our comfort zones. I knew before I left the house that day that there was no reason to skate other than the act itself, yet I had tried to force honor out of a day that should've been about getting comfortable on my board again, not trying to punch above my weight toward some projected enlightenment. This is the reason I gasp at new scooter owners going twenty-five miles per hour down congested streets at the squeeze of a handlebar, without knowing what a fall and failure feel like. They might as well drive those things blindfolded, and skating the Oak Tech banks with a stiff, buzzed body felt similarly foolish. I jogged for the first time a month later, on the trails at Mount Davidson in San Francisco, cresting to the massive cross acquired by a local group to commemorate victims of the Armenian genocide. I managed to walk around enough to meet my parents in town for a trip to the Monet exhibit at the de Young. I even gained enough mobility to have dinner with my girlfriend in downtown Oakland before going on a walk and proposing to her on the east side of Lake Merritt. I can still feel how much that knee hurt as we turned and took selfies, smiles from ear to ear.

And I wonder still if that dude's play went well at Oak Tech and if the kids received a standing ovation.

3.

WILD IN THE STREETS

Fireworks would end the night. It didn't matter if we'd see them. What mattered was getting back on BART before the last eastbound train from San Francisco and not getting stuck at the Transbay Terminal, waiting on the late-night Owl bus back to downtown Oakland that crawled through every local stop before getting close to our place near Lake Merritt.

My roommate C and I had been navigating this challenge since we met in 2002 at the UC Berkeley dorms. We quickly started going to shows together, visiting for the first time venues we had previously only read about—and sometimes for the last time, if the venue shuttered afterward. Finding shows, this is what C and I knew best, having grown up on different sides of Los Angeles County. Me, on its eastern fringe in Pomona. C, in South LA's South Gate before settling in nearby Paramount. Still strangers then, we were both unknowingly scouring the same *Los Angeles Times* calendar-section pages, visualizing our sonic obsessions in text and photos, the bands and concerts we heard about on 106.7 FM KROQ's nightly countdown, the Furious Five at nine. We grew up triangulating actual journalism against rumors from older kids—the ones with patches on their thrifted workmen's shirts—and against our own imaginations of what band would play where and with what set list.

Once we arrived in NorCal, we went straight to the back pages of the *SF Weekly*, *San Francisco Examiner*, and *East Bay Express* or to the flyers at Amoeba Music, figuring out how to navigate the city before we could even order a drink. We were bringing to life a world we couldn't envision in SoCal, one in which our feet were destined for subways and buses and not the floors of friends' cars, and we were emancipated from having to ask for a ride to access anything we cared about.

Too much of Southern Californian life starts at sixteen. The acquisition of a driver's license provides a ticket to an intentionally paved world; for us in the San Gabriel Valley, it provided the ability to see shows downtown, in Hollywood, or sometimes in Orange County. Cars seemed like a nuisance in the Bay Area, and I loved that. I loved knowing a skateboard was a worthy vehicle here, something that could go down one of the city's notoriously steep hills, test the limits, and (hopefully) survive the flight down and through traffic, daring those red lights to turn green upon a skater's fast-paced, downhill arrival. Pedestrians, like skaters, navigate spaces dictated to them, making a space, like a city or neighborhood, their own through a self-made path. The space is carved by a body's responses to an area divided by the desire of direction multiplied by necessity. Even the etymology of *routine* points to *route*: a pathway, a navigation of a relationship within a space, a limitless city with a terrifying topography of hills and cliffs.

It's the Fourth of July 2007. Two liberal arts degrees and zero careers later, we are now smarter, snarkier, more impulsive versions of our dormitory selves and still timing our mad sprints from the Fillmore or, bolder yet, from the Independent on Divisadero all the way back to the Civic Center BART station. I can feel the tule fog cool inside my lungs, legs blindly jogging through the parks off Gough, the side streets toward Van Ness, and that glowing escalator in the sky next to Burger King at Eighth and Market.

C and I were living in downtown Oakland with a friend from the student co-op we'd shared with twenty others through most of undergrad. The three of us spent our time across as many bedrooms, with the recession fast approaching. Our degrees felt meaningless, placeholders for a sense of accomplishment increasingly out of reach.

C didn't skate. I'd had zero skater friends in college. My friends were poets or indie kids from the co-ops, culturally overlapping with skateboarding's allied spaces—footwear, music, fashion, marijuana, art. I spent most afternoons skating the neighborhood and nearby Chinatown solo. Flatground sessions in Madison Square Park next to the Lake Merritt BART, one of the city's original public parks. Pushing down Webster to Jack London Square's warehouses. I still love skating the ledge above the Posey Tube, the four-stairs-up-four-stairs-down ledge with the built-in angle iron on its side at the top of the underground tunnel that leads to the island of Alameda.

If we headed to San Francisco, it'd be toward the Mission, to Dolores Park, eating Panchita's pupusas and waiting for the pedestrian weed-edible vendor known as the Truffle Man. Corner-store trips and Arinell Pizza–barstool blackouts. We could pull off weekday respectability enough to consistently work office temp jobs, but I'll never forget C in the kitchen one night, cooking and staring at me as I sat on the kitchen floor on our recycling crate upturned into a quasi chair: "You look like a rat."

"A what?"

"A skate rat. Look at you."

I looked. My shoes were torn from kickflips, the sides' thin canvas blown out from ollies and a growing hole in the sole of my left shoe from pushing across Lake Merritt every morning. A random graphic tee held it all somewhat together with an arbitrary beanie worn indoors.

The years after college were when skating started feeling good again. It felt like I had the right, the time, and some income to figure out how to balance it with work, dating, maybe even writing—actual adulthood. My body, aware of itself in ways a pubescent boy shockingly isn't, felt capable. It realized that the question wasn't *whether* I still skated but *how* I continued to skate and grow alongside the toy, the endorphin tool, that didn't keep me a child but placed me in communication with its root definitions of joy.

Events made that joy a shared experience. I started going to more demos and events around the Bay produced by *Thrasher*, local companies, or visiting teams such as Emerica Shoes. Emerica had set off on the Wild Tour, a two-week journey from Washington culminating in Wild in the Streets, a permitted Fourth of July takeover of San Francisco's Embarcadero. The tour kicked off on June 21 for Go Skateboarding Day, orchestrated by Emerica's distributor Sole Technology, in which skaters "take over" the streets en masse on the same day, worldwide. Wild in the Streets was a San Francisco version of Go Skateboarding Day. This was my plan for the Fourth in 2007—skate by day, go to the show with C at night.

Both Go Skateboarding Day and Wild in the Streets were inspired by the popular monthly cycling event Critical Mass. Though its roots are Swiss, Critical Mass was popularized in the early 1990s by San Francisco cycling enthusiasts, who cycled together on the last Friday of every month on streets otherwise designated for cars and buses. The gathering had a come-one, come-all approach, with the only requirements being you and a bicycle, and many used the events to advocate for cyclist rights, including bike lanes along popular city thoroughfares. Critical Mass proved that a city could stop at the organized calls of a mobile, non-car constituency. As the need for skateparks and their construction increased throughout the decade, skateboarding events proved its popularity. And while Critical Mass was a more frequent affair, events like Wild in the Streets and Go Skateboarding Day similarly created a shared calendar for all skaters to plan around.

C and I had moved from Southern California to the Bay Area for a carless existence—and people wanted more of it. There was a growing sense of pedestrian and cyclist rights, of taking streets back and away from cars or, at the very least, deemphasizing their priority. Bike lanes were not nearly as widely proliferated as they are today, and a bike lane would often simply consist of painted arrows reiterating the existing fact that cyclists can share the road with cars. Part of navigating the Bay still means using cyclists' terms for specific bike-friendly and pedestrian paths.

The most notable is the Wiggle connecting Duboce Park

with the greater Church and Market district, public transportation, and access to nearby neighborhoods like the Mission District, Noe Valley, and the Castro. The term was formalized in 1994 in the cycling newsletter *The Tubular Times*, and the physical path of the Wiggle dates to the Indigenous Ohlone tribes, for whom Church and Market Streets led to water sources near Duboce Park. The Wiggle exists not only on Native land but on their paths as well.

Taking over city streets every last Friday of the month was one way the San Francisco Bicycle Coalition actively fought for bike lanes like the Wiggle and other bike-friendly paths, a fight that spread through Coalition messaging but mainly through word of mouth. Skaters took note.

————

As Southern Californian skate publications grappled with staff departures (*Transworld Skateboarding*), new indie upstarts (*The Skateboard Mag*), and other relevant publications (*Skateboarder Magazine*), *Thrasher* was investing in Bay Area–specific events and increasingly web-friendly content. As all skate publications debated how to support themselves with advertisements, with *Transworld* wrestling with ads as far from skateboarding's core as the Marines and Right Guard deodorant, *Thrasher* willingly allied with the Boost Mobiles and Arnette eyewears of the world to produce amazing contest series. For example, Skate Rock, where skaters do demos by day and play in bands at the skatepark at night, increased its presence in the late 2000s, with corporate shoe brands like Converse footing the bill. Supporting skate teams and the skate DVDs that came free with issues of *Thrasher* allowed otherwise-background skaters to come to the forefront of the industry. Always and forever a magazine, more than any skate publication at the time, *Thrasher* was turning itself into a platform connecting all generations of skateboarders.

The mid-2000s rise of hipster culture crossed over with Emerica's extremely cool team. They embodied the kind of rocker-meets-thrift-store cool that enabled them to ride Harleys, date musicians, and be photographed wearing not skate shoes but dress shoes, with many of their riders spending more time in bars than on the board as the decade progressed. The Emerica pros, amateurs, filmers, and friends made the Wild Ride journey from Washington to San Francisco in Sprinter vans and as a motorcycle gang.

Emerica's relevance was at its zenith, sponsoring some of skateboarding's biggest generational talents. Their tours consisted of doing demos by day and filming on the streets at night, as the team and brand were building to the 2009 release of their full-length video *Stay Gold*. Considered the last big skate video of its time, with the rise of social media perceived as a threat to skate videos' profitability, the film, directed by Jon Miner, featured Andrew Reynolds, Emerica's marquee pro and former *Thrasher* Skater of the Year. With multiple pro-model shoes for Emerica, a clothing company called Altamont, and his skateboard brand, Baker, Reynolds earned himself the reputable nickname "The Boss" early in his career.

But unlike for the younger Emerica riders, this was no Wild Ride for him but a professional tour: doing demos, filming missions, signing autographs for kids. He'd nearly died in a drunk driving incident, his car lodging between two trees after veering off-road while blackout drunk in Florida. Now, as Emerica's and Baker's elder statesman, his newfound focus was on a healthier regimen and amazing tricks. That was the number one reason many attended an Emerica demo: to bear witness to the Boss and the flick of his front foot when executing his signature frontside kickflips.

Later that year, the VICE web show *Epicly Later'd* highlighted the motorcycle accidents experienced on different parts of the tour by those who chose Harleys over a tour bus. Even at a time when members of the team legendarily turned sober, slowly engendering a generation of health-conscious skaters to follow, VICE's footage shows younger riders clearly still in their dive-bar phase. Still, the team's intergenerational-legend status was nearly a decade deep by 2007, with little having changed in the team's lineup since their inaugural video, *This Is Skateboarding*, was released in 2003 after two years of production and hype. In this sense, just being at Wild Ride as an onlooker was like rubbing shoulders with skaters who were more than the culture they represented.

They were documented by the creator of *Epicly Later'd*, photographer Patrick O'Dell, whose personal website EpiclyLaterd.com had inspired the VICE web show. A former *Thrasher* staff photographer, O'Dell had moved to New York at a time when the downtown-Manhattan scene was popping off. The website showed skaters not skating. Not skating meant partying. Going on road trips without boards. Hosting their own DJ nights. Attending gallery openings and fashion shows. Playing in bands and releasing music, however terrible. They took photos and published zines. Went to Morrissey shows and jumped onstage to hug the singer before being escorted off by security. EpiclyLaterd.com crystallized what it meant to build a life around the things you cared about and to document it all.

I'd refresh my browser at the end of each day, and the same black screen would stare back with its simple title and a left-justified row of white hyperlinks with text usually from song lyrics or skate-video references, hyperlinked clues like cryptic notes to a friend. The web series brought O'Dell's website to life and created one of the better nonfiction cinematic portrayals of skateboarding culture ever—even equipping C with the term *skate rat*.

One of O'Dell's recurring characters was Jerry Hsu, one of my favorite skaters, whose career trajectory I witnessed upon introduction to the culture. A year before the Wild Ride tour, Hsu released one of skateboarding's greatest individual skate parts for the inaugural video of his board sponsor, Enjoi, titled *Bag of Suck*. If skate-video parts are the micro-short-film equivalents of an album, this was Hsu's *Songs in the Key of Life*. He worked quietly and tirelessly on his closing part for years, a two-song-long opus that put him in contention for the illustrious Skater of the Year and, at the very least, certified him as one of the greatest street skaters of his generation.

In a *Thrasher* article celebrating the video's fifteenth anniversary, Kyle Caramillo recounted filming with Hsu on weekends for his part. "Friday night I would hit up Jerry and make plans for Saturday. Jerry would go to a spot and get his trick or he would destroy himself. And if he did his trick fast, we would go to the next spot. Monday through Thursday he wouldn't skate; it was like he was dead. He killed himself every weekend."

O'Dell documented *Bag of Suck*'s release on his website. The premiere was in San Jose in March of my last semester of college. I had no car or idea how close the venue was to Amtrak, plus college, so I refreshed the blog even more often that week for a peek into one of the most anticipated films of that year. The premiere was chaotic: skaters were kicked out of the theater, beers were massively distributed mid-movie, there were altercations with police, and Enjoi was left with fines to pay. And the rumors were true: Jerry Hsu indeed had an amazing last part—the highest honor for a skater in a skate video, the "curtains" of the production—and *Bag of Suck* was an instant classic from a skate team that never published skateboarding in its ads but instead party photos and dumb one-liners.

Today, scrolling through the website's archives, everyone looks wildly young. The red-eye effect is present in everyone's faces from the era's compact-digital-camera flashes. Like O'Dell himself, the blog was rooted in skateboarding and in showing it from a different perspective, the angles skaters are most curious about: Pulling up in random parts of the country to go to specific bands' shows. Making non-skater but as-cool-as-skater friends in your twenties. Going to the bar constantly. A lot of these skaters would thankfully go sober. Some are the exact same now as they were when they were documented in the mid-2000s.

Demos are often a kid's first taste of the skateboard industry: Meeting pros and seeing skateboarding at a high level go down by design. A performance of sorts, or a real-time product-marketing tour. A team with enough of a budget to rent or own a van, usually from a board or shoe company, visits skate shops and does a demonstration of the team's skateboarding abilities for the local scene for free. Stickers and product tosses from the event sponsors are always a key incentive for a kid, hungry for any official skateboarding ephemera to find and collect like treasure. The companies hope that exposure to their brands, if not to skateboarding in general, will lead a kid to buy their product at the skate shop hosting the demo. Some demos take place at school assemblies, though most are hosted by local skate shops on weekends, usually the shops with big accounts with the touring brands. In a pre-internet society, this was a key way to see and understand skaters and how they're pulling off their tricks. This was before social media turned a previously unseen lifestyle into branded content. Before behind-the-scenes edits of video parts were taken for granted, before the final, best tricks of someone's video parts were leaked online. Demos were part of the analog presentation of skateboarding, which included VHS, skate magazines, and word of mouth.

It's hard to gauge how big a demo is going to be. Some feel like backyard sessions while others feel like ticketed events. Across the spectrum, pros arrive and skate a skatepark or a makeshift course created by the skate shop, or they bring their own situation if there's a budget. The team skates, ideally showing off some cool tricks to gets the kids hyped, and then they do a signing and throw free crap out to the crowd. But the goal is to see your favorite pro skate. Sure, we the viewers are not watching them land monumental tricks for skate videos, settling for the contained environment of a skatepark, but we relish the opportunity to understand how fast a favorite pro skates, or how short or tall they actually are, or how high their ollies really appear in person, the things that videos can't fully articulate. Videos present perfect lands and noninjurious falls to create an ideal utopia of a session; seeing it in person pulls back the veil to reveal the muscled psychosis and psychic granularity required to skate at a high level.

On July 3, the day before Wild in the Streets in San Francisco, the Emerica team did a demo in the East Bay at Berkeley's skatepark. A massive tour bus and small Sprinter vans dotted a Berkeley neighborhood where warehouses rubbed rusty by the Pacific were transitioning into market-rate live-work lofts. The bus was wrapped in Boost Mobile branding, explaining those oddly placed ads in magazines, everyone vying for their slice of the youth market. It conveyed the scale of the tour and the idolatry that could follow.

I showed up alone with my board and zero intention of skating the park, just transporting myself from BART to the park and demonstrating that, indeed, I am a skater. Because official introductions between pros and "kids" are rare outside of a signing and always odd to attend if you're not a teenager, I didn't really know why I was there other than to see an exhibition of some of the best, biggest names in skateboarding. Many attendees still had braces, others were dropped off by their parents, many harassing the pros upon arrival for an autograph, for free products. Other kids charged the skatepark, disregarding the fact that it was a demo, joining the show before slowly realizing they were out of their league.

Somehow I ended up standing next to O'Dell near the fence surrounding the skatepark. We made eye contact and he said hi, not so much in an *I am being recognized* kind of way but more in a *You are still staring at me, hello?* kind of way. I was as stoned as I was insecure and immediately replied with a hi and a knee-jerk question not about him, his photography, or his experience on the trip but about a zine Emerica was publishing with a photographer that wasn't even O'Dell, who, confused, said he didn't know when the zine was coming out and smartly walked away. He walked over to Jerry Hsu, my favorite skater, surely relaying this odd story, likely one of several follies they experienced on their trip, and laughing not so much at my expense but at my social reality in that moment.

Which is fine. It is what it is, the unstructured social milieu through which any subculture operates. I was just the latest to falter when the facts were pretty clear. We're at a demo. Try not to get hit by a board and watch the great and soon-to-be-great skaters you may never see again. I didn't stay for the signing, swallowed the remnants of my pride after my social interactions, and went back to Oakland, knowing the Fourth of July event was still to come.

———

The Wild in the Streets event on the Fourth of July was the final day of Emerica's Wild Ride tour. The meetup event was at Ferry Plaza just across the street from the Ferry Building, or, as skaters refer to the plaza, the Island. The pedestrian-friendly path and plaza divide the streetcars from the Ferry Building and guide pedestrians to the beginning of Market Street.

The Island was the previous site of the Embarcadero Freeway, built in the late 1950s as part of the urban renewal that destroyed the Western Addition and the Fillmore's Black communities but allowed for car owners to play the game of suburban flight and find their way into and out of their financial-district, waterfront jobs. The freeway wrapped around Justin Herman

Plaza and its signature Vaillancourt Fountain and split itself in two at the foot of the massive Alcoa Building, the headquarters of the Aluminum Company of America, which boomed after World War II.

The path of the freeway would hint at legendary skate spots to come. Indeed, if you follow the freeway's old paths, all of the city's spots appear at the terminus of Market Street and at the waterfront: Pier 7's short ledges with metallic tops and smooth ground. The Bay Blocks, formerly the Embarcadero Art Ribbon, a string of cheap concrete ledges shaped like extremely harsh chairs, with short, elevated backs in the middle that had nice green glass bricks in the center. These bricks would apparently light up when it was first installed, hence *ribbon*, but they quickly fell victim to irreparable water damage, dooming the project. And designer Lawrence Halprin's projects: the Hubba Hideout ledges at the Alcoa Building pedestrian bridge and the most famous, Justin Herman Plaza, or what would become known as Embarco to skaters and, particularly from 1991 to 1994, would be home to the most progressive examples of street skateboarding in the world.

Halprin's spots had his trademark floors made of red bricks. He designed much of the city after leaders recognized urban renewal's failure to engage the city and aimed instead to civically engage with public-space redesigns, with Halprin helming the United Nations Civic Center, Ghirardelli Square at Fisherman's Wharf, and Justin Herman Plaza at the Embarcadero. The sound of wheels across these bricks is a subtle thunder that sonically moves only forward, no stop in sight.

In 1976, Halprin joined a team that updated and landscaped a nearby park bridging the distance between Justin Herman

Plaza and the Alcoa Building, creating the pedestrian bridge from the building, over Davis Street, and into a new pedestrian plaza that would become known by skaters worldwide as Hubba Hideout. The Alcoa Building would eventually mark the spot for skaters, who would find there a pedestrian bridge with two brutalist concrete handrails going down six stairs into the small, out-of-sight plaza with Halprin's red bricks, guiding pedestrians toward the Embarcadero waterfront—and distracting people from the massive double-decker freeway.

The Embarcadero Freeway met its end around its fortieth birthday with the Loma Prieta earthquake, its upper decks collapsing into the lower tiers, like the tragedies in Oakland on Interstate 880 and the Bay Bridge. It was approved for demolition in a 6–5 vote and gone by 1991. Part of its boulevard replacement was Harry Bridges Plaza in front of the Ferry Building, which was a stop for the streetcars traveling along the Embarcadero. It quickly became a skate spot, the smooth dark ground providing ample room for practicing flatground flip tricks. Two octagonal pillars made of California granite face each other and allow pedestrians to sit and skaters to skate. Large chest-high spheres dot the plaza's edges, dividing pedestrians from cars driving south toward the Bay Bridge. Finished in 2001, the plaza was named after union leader Harry Bridges, who led the maritime strike at the Port of San Francisco for nearly ninety days in 1934.

The Island was the latest in a myriad of historically significant downtown San Francisco street spots. It was big enough and central enough to start the descent to New Spot, way south of the Bay Bridge down Third Street in the Dogpatch. That day, randoms started skating upturned trash cans and loose signage scattered around the plaza's flatground, while pedestrians tried to walk unharmed from the Ferry Building toward Market Street. Some of the younger sponsored pros and amateurs got into the mix, while the older pros milled about on the sideline in the shade, before a cringeworthy group photo.

In the photo, all the skaters are near the Island ledges, holding our boards precariously above our heads. Mine is a Baker skateboard with artwork done by the graffiti artist Neck Face. I wanted to be seen in the photo, I remember, and was bummed later when I couldn't find myself in the event-recap photos published to one of the sponsor's websites. I was twenty-two. What did any of us expect to happen that day? Meet the pros, share joints together, ask for autographs from the older, sober pros?

One big reason I wanted to attend was to explore a place I hadn't before as a skater, with other skaters who shared my perspective on physical space. Part of showing up was to see if the event was even legal (it was) and whether the cops would escort skaters along the Embarcadero (they did). Skating down Third Street was a quick reminder that things can go wrong. We headed south, SFPD motorcycles blocking traffic as a bunch of kids took off under the Bay Bridge toward the Giants ballpark. Amid the crowd, you could tell where sections of MUNI rail were interrupting the concrete by the ripples of skaters quickly ollieing over the tracks or grabbing their boards and running the distance across the tracks, fearing their wheels getting caught, falling, and causing a pileup. The pros were smarter, staying off Third and sticking to the sidewalks, others hitching rides on the organizers' golf carts. Past the Giants ballpark and McCovey Cove, we continued down Third Street along a stretch of warehouses and empty lots, all now long gone, toward the newest skate spot at the time in San Francisco, the aptly titled New Spot, also known as Third and Army.

Nestled alongside Islais Creek, between the 280 freeway overpass and Third Street, New Spot is a long, skinny collection of concrete ledges topped by thick tubes. Notoriously windy, the spot afforded skaters the opportunity to do lines— sequences of landed tricks in succession—with ledges on either side of a straight smooth path offering nothing but options. At New Spot's entrance, a large planter that resembled a ten-stair greeted skaters. They turned the planter into a gap, balancing on a skinny runway toward the top of the planter and doing tricks from the top to the bottom over the space between. It was difficult enough that there were still tricks that hadn't been landed at this gap, opportunities for aspiring skaters to make their name and do something unique here to leave their literal mark on the spot.

The gap soon took center stage. The young flow riders began hucking themselves down the gap as the known names started from the top. The tall, lanky, goofy-footed flow kid perfectly executed a 360 flip, while a household name did his signature hardflip down the gap as effortlessly as in the videos. With sunglasses on too—that confidence.

And between and beyond those two skaters, another older, seemingly career amateur continued to battle a trick that he could flick, catch, and land—but couldn't roll away from. I say *older* when he was probably just closer to his mid-twenties than some of the other riders. He appeared grizzled, weathered, but ready to battle a trick that, initially, he seemed to have in the bag. It's a bigspin kickflip—the body moves 180 degrees

as your board does a 360 kickflip—and has the visual effect
of a motion-graphic peacock quickly sprouting its feathers. A
lot is happening beneath a skater's feet, and speed is lost in
the process—which doesn't bode well for trying to take off and
over a tall, large gap and roll away with some amount of speed.
Add a skinny runway, and the math needed to land the trick
was more than average—and that's the point.

Since his body turned 180 degrees in the backside direction, every fall propelled him straight backward onto his lower
back, repeatedly. Some initial near makes sparked a fire under him to commit to the battle and try over and over, slamming until his thrifted Harley Davidson T-shirt was shredded
beyond its potential resale value. The crowd watched, hoping
for the make that demos are made for, but such demos take
place at skateparks designed for an achievement to become a
routine, mechanized, perfected triumph. Here we were in the
streets, at an actual uncontrollable street spot.

Time is a skater's worst enemy. It became clear he wasn't
going to land it. Not that day, at least. He'd have to come
back—which, I imagine, as a touring skater is painful enough,
the audience not helping this skater's nerves any. Because however much he is fulfilling the job of skating the demos and being part of the tour, he is not maximizing the tour without
the land, the photo, the coverage to prove it—and the subsequent paycheck, upgrade of sponsorship status, and chance of
a pro career. Younger, less haggard skaters can do similar, if
not better, tricks over and down the gap and try these tricks
for longer periods of time. Skateboarding is a service industry where all we serve are projected good times, the proverbial
bros, and land tricks within a handful of tries. Here, in front of

everyone, was the reality: someone close to my age realizing, firsthand, it wasn't happening that day.

I would have felt bad if it weren't for the fact that I admired the honesty in him giving us that session, that effort, not for failure but to witness the tries, to see how hard it is to land a trick and make it look mature and not a flailing display of pubescent limbs.

This wasn't the worst of spots or environments to not land a trick in public. A year or so later I'd attend a *Thrasher*-sponsored event called Bust or Bail at Paul Revere Elementary in San Francisco's Bernal Heights, featuring a massive sixteen-stair handrail going down the center, with skaters doing tricks down the rail and over the stairs, and even tricks out and over both, all off the strength of an hour-long weekend permit and some DIY construction to make the roll-up to the staircase rideable. Jake Phelps was on the mic, holding court, excoriating anyone in sight that he chose.

After they played Hendrix's "The Star-Spangled Banner" over the PA, the second skater tried something backside down the handrail, clipped the rail, lost control of his board, and fell collarbone-first and headfirst straight to the bottom of the set. This type of slam, one so brutal but so commonly associated with skating a large handrail, has a name in skateboarding coined by Phelps himself, who screamed it into the microphone pretty much upon the skater's impact: "Scorpion!" A perfect description, legs over head, curling over the body as the skater's face cheesegraters the pavement.

That was the first official trick of the session/contest. The crowd was shook. Phelps was scream-laughing from the adrenaline and the visual chaos he helped create. Photographers sat huddled at the bottom of the stairs, hats backward to block the sun and maybe even the spit from the foaming mouths of skaters like me oohing and aahing at everything going down at this set that we'd only seen tackled at this skill level in skate videos.

The sun was setting on the Fourth of July, there was less skating, and more fireworks explosions were being heard across the city. Off to the side, some random kids were teasing one of the members of the crew for hooking up with a skater the night or two before over by a concrete Jersey barrier. Whatever after-after-party would occur on this hot summer holiday was going to be nuts, and unsurprisingly, everyone headed toward Dolores Park. I wondered which weed-edible opportunist would be hustling that day and how well they'd do on a big tourist weekend. I walked back up toward Embarcadero along the bay. The Giants were out of town but everyone was still out on the warm streets. I had to get back to downtown Oakland, drop off my board, and meet up with C to head back to the city for a show at the Independent.

The show's lineup spanned most of the spectrum of contemporary metal: thrash (Wolves in the Throne Room), stoner Sabbath worship (Weedeater), and drone (the pioneers, Earth, and Sunn O)))). This was C's scene and not mine, or maybe it was, considering that growing up watching Zero Skateboards videos in the late 1990s was a lesson in Black Sabbath's discography, and other brands' videos introduced me to Cymande, Jimmy Cliff, and Gang Starr. Across the four bands at the show, the historically fuzzed ripple effects of their shade of metal frantically sped up or slowed to a riff-focused sludge, or the even slower, louder, fully extended notes of Sunn O))) that hung in the thick weed-smoke sky accumulating above us.

The crowd was a little older than at the skate event, closer to a late-twenties-to-early-thirties crowd, but I wondered if anyone made it to the earlier events and skated all afternoon before coming here. Going to shows and skateboarding came around the same time for me, finding the spaces on the street and the venues that mattered to me because I knew each space contained a world view, an understanding of what we all collectively want to experience or bear witness to. Across a city on a holiday like the Fourth, so many were searching for that same feeling within their own spaces and nooks of the city, rooftops in the avenues, or a literal square foot of space in Dolores Park. Cities are invitations to parts of ourselves we've always known but can't access without such introductions.

C and I played it safe on the Fourth and left a few songs into headliner Sunn O)))'s set, still running across town to the Civic Center BART, our Burger King beacon savior, cutting across the plaza in front of city hall. Still, the brief bearing of witness to the cloaked, smoke-machined, marijuana-propelled duo left an intense, lasting impression: the sonic boom of the dual guitar attack, fuzzed distortion, and beyond-residentially-permitted feedback considerations. The sound stretches and bends as much as it haunts the bodies melting in its presence, some unnecessarily bobbing full throttle, always standing toward the front of the stage, but most trying to keep their chins up, if only to find cool air amid this temporal humidifier of flesh and exhaled cannabis and residual holiday bonfire and barbeque smells alike. Like most of Sunn O)))'s set, a single slow note was strummed into the air like a declaration, or a sheet of metal welded to the top of a windy flagpole. The following morning's *SFGate* write-up was kinder than their forewarning tone days earlier. It recapped the Wild in the Streets event positively, noting the organization, staff organizers, and more than a dozen officers present. The article noted that then lieutenant Mike Cleary summed up the skate event as "peaceful—no problems."

C moved a few years later to Los Angeles and we talk daily, because it's not Mars, though the Bay Area bubble says as much. While I was writing this, he moved again with his family to Oklahoma, which by California-bubble standards *is* Mars. I'm not sure what the venue-to-public-transportation ratio looks like there, but I imagine it doesn't have to cross a bay, a sliver of the Pacific Ocean, anytime soon. We've spent more years apart than together at this point, but wherever either of us is, we give each other updates from a pedestrian point of view: the way the buses screw up, the billboards from opportunistic lawyers, whether a flier for a Shen Yun production reaches wherever we are. But I'm thankful it's those years we shared.

And on that Fourth, within whatever degree of independence and freedom we gave ourselves permission to explore, did everyone's spit and blood and sex and ruin and resin hits and exhalations feel as hot to the touch as those bombs bursting in smoke-filled air? Or was it just the feeling of not making it as a pro skater, body slammed and public all the same, this twenty-four-hour exhibition of bodies and flags waving at one another like a pointless hypnosis, waiting for the sky to tell us a story we hear only once a year? We didn't witness America's glory in the skies, the violence of bombs and their fantastic mirage color coated to dazzle. It was another night of trying to synchronize ourselves to a city's rhythm for the opportunity to collectively bear witness to everything a city can create. Some measure the degree of debauchery more than others. From city-sanctioned hangouts to Dolores Park becoming a demilitarized zone of fireworks, beautiful views, and chaos, it felt like everyone was part of San Francisco's story that night, trying to navigate a space defined by everything we are not supposed to do.

Like C and I fleeing from whatever subways were telling us how to spend our nights. It's a challenge the flat clock of time guides us through with its hands: How much can you do in such mortal hours, how much can you experience, taste, lust for, and achieve? How do you stretch these seconds, hours, weeks, to make something out of dust, this time we, as strangers, share in the streets? Like this very city itself, an empire that paved sand dunes into a metropolis. It is this energy, looking back, that is the inertia to our memories, our shared experiences, the unseen marks of every city screaming back to the sky and its bombastic technicolor outfit, we too are here.

What did you do on the Fourth of July? they'll ask at the water cooler, and will any answer include those drops of blood shed on the pavement, the histories paved and hiding us civilized folks away from those foot-carved paths on Ohlone land?

4.

NO LURK LIMIT

Inserting a skate-video VHS into the family video console felt intrinsically renegade. The black brick holding together the magnetized video tape might as well have been a Girls Gone Wild video or something equally salacious and unregulated. Before smartphones and online video, watching skate videos on the same console on which my parents watched *60 Minutes* was akin to trying to carve out some privacy to watch scrambled clips of the Playboy Channel. Maybe it was the decade in which skate videos entered our home that made them feel part of this larger underground culture of downtown–Los Angeles raves, car races, and music scenes amid a mainstream, televised MTV of everything from safe-sex awareness to voter-registration programming.

Skateboarding's most representative and labor-intensive presentation is the skate video. If a band's four-vinyl, gatefold mega-album were a skate video, it'd be a thirty-minute compression of a dozen individual parts, with each skater's part its own two-to-three-minute solo project. An accumulation of years' worth of work for just a few seconds of documented tricks—"clips"—sequenced, compressed, and shared across digital platforms onto a skater's glowing screen. If skate magazines' still photography offers questions about the form's possibilities, skate videos present the answers at full speed or in slow-motion homage: the proof is the movement and sonics behind every landed (or failed) trick.

Skaters exist in a unique, intersectional cultural universe whose slang, fashion, and skate spots are discovered in magazines and skate videos. The hieroglyphics of skate-company logos, shoe brands, upstart clothing brands, and more become part of a new world that skate videos bring to life. The interstitial moments between sessions, when skaters tease each other, pull pranks, interact with pedestrians, observe the world around them—and do the tricks—opened the streets up to kids like me too young to explore them. And while a magazine may capture a moment in time, nothing can help you visualize it more than hearing skateboarding at full volume.

Skate videos are passports to the world's skateboarding opens. From the pants, the shoulders leading to a well-popped maneuver, and the soundtrack to the angle of the cameras and the light flares—it all adds to the spectacle skateboarding offers through visualized demonstration. This is how you skate. This is how you should look rolling away, escaping death, arrest, or both. What if being a basketball fan meant no longer watching LeBron on TV but only seeing LeBron train in the gym? There's an energy, a passion, missing in such spaces that is palpable particularly when presented through video.

Growing up, I hypermemorized as many skate videos as possible. Every new song became a portal to a new band, record label, or genre of music. In a prestreaming world, skate videos were unintentional mixtapes. Brands were defined by their soundtracks and tastes, finding songs tasteful enough to soundtrack a skater's part. That part doesn't even have to be that good; the song can act as a savior, a literal redemption song for otherwise lackluster parts, preventing someone from smashing the fast-forward button on the remote control.

Skate spots became visually memorized through their frequent appearances in skate videos. With usually only one filmer and several skaters to shoot, famous spots like Lockwood Elementary in Los Angeles or LOVE Park in Philadelphia were introduced through cameos. This allowed the viewer to see how skaters were skating and filming together, landing tricks on the same day in the same sessions (as told by their corresponding outfits), helping us understand the mechanics of being a sponsored skater making a skate video.

Over time, skaters build a global map of skate spots famous for their appearances in videos. Show me a well-skated ledge from the other side of the Atlantic and I can tell you whether it's the dark marble from Barcelona's MACBA, the classic, white, curved beauty at Milano Station, or the graffitied and preserved glory of Southbank Centre's historic London car park. Play Sonic Youth's "Titanium Expose" right now and I could tell you the tricks, in sequence, that Ed Templeton executes in the 1996 classic *Welcome to Hell*.

Today, skate videos are part of online content, the daily queue governing our lives' entertainment. Still, skate videos continue to be published online using the traditional format of individual parts bookended by a montage intro and a B-roll outro in the credits. The internet hasn't killed the "long-form" VHS skate-produced skate video; in fact, it's helped the technology, production, and publication of videos advance. From independent edits to branded productions, an abundance of online skate content has helped quell the fear that social media's rise would mark the death of the full-length skate video as a medium. And while I don't know if parts are as memorized by today's youth as they were in my generation, how can the music, tricks, spots, and pedestrian run-ins that the world's skate videos embody not map the same things onto skaters' minds today as they did onto mine in 1996?

Through my twenties I'd watch skate videos so frequently it was like background music at a bar, and some bars owned by skaters indeed play videos with or without music all night, the tricks and slams bombastic enough to stun strangers while acting as private love letters to skaters who might knowingly hum the songs to themselves from their barstools. Sure, the sight of a big handrail trick can be jaw-dropping, but it's the environments that house the tricks—the architecture, the cities, the nature of the pedestrians and how they respond to seeing skateboarding produced and documented at this level ("How do they follow them?" is a frequent pedestrian question)—that open up the world of skateboarding through documentation.

Skate videos need the streets to prove the alchemy of their cinematic form, and neither private nor public skateparks will ever capture this. Private skateparks like the Berrics morphed into content factories, fueling an ad-heavy website with muscle-supplement-authored mission statements: "There's nothing special about dying. Anyone can do that. Push the future." Primitive Skateboards' new private park is seemingly media-day lit for the 'Gram, where the stairs even light up for flair. In the age of content, YouTube channels like Braille circumvented core cultural platforms (and respect) in favor of a direct-to-consumer, click-to-subscribe model. It's telling that the first question a Google search for Braille generates is "Why do skaters hate Braille?" I'd answer that it's because Braille creates more content curated around personalities rather than video parts in conversation—structurally and visually—with their historical precedents.

Today skate videos may premiere on YouTube, with skaters worldwide hosting their own watch parties in the wake of the pandemic, but many are still published to VHS, DVD, and other Luddite formats in addition to streaming. Australia's Pass-Port Skateboards' deluxe edition of its video *Kitsch* was a custom-shaped USB drive tucked inside a full-color wall-size silk scarf wrapped in a palm-size box.

The packaging and nuances of a video's release underscore the core drive of skate videos: to showcase a collective's vision of skateboarding through the filmer's direction and the creativity of the skaters in the streets—and for some brands, through advertisements. Skate magazines demonstrate monthly how advertising fuels the presentation of skateboarding, with each new print ad introducing a new rider or showcasing a new trick done for the first time ever in a famous, iconic skate spot. Palace Skateboards flips that motif on its head and stretches its boundaries—leveraging digital content for sixty-minute skate videos and short, barely one-minute advertisements for one-off collaborations with some of fashion's most regarded brands, while somehow always keeping the skate team in the frame of the picture.

I love to binge Palace's YouTube channel, divided across two playlists—ADVERTS and SKATEBOARDING. Instead of trying to cross over with American skaters and buyers, Palace

reconfigured the power dynamics of the skateboarding industry by focusing on its crew, city, and sounds. Its skate videos
show London's finest skaters skating at the best spots in the
world to a mash-up of 1990s rave classics, while Palace also
releases collaborative twelve-inch records with Detroit deep
house legend Theo Parrish. It's produced entire ad campaigns
with short witty commercials for vanguard brands like Cal-
vin Klein, sports teams like Juventus, superstars like Sir Elton
John (who proclaimed, "The bitch is back!" holding up a shirt
with his image and Palace's wordmark), brands like Polo, and
institutions like the Tate Modern. Palace itself is rooted in the
shared spaces of not just skate spots but terrible small apartments: the crew of friends—the Palace Wayward Boys Choir—
called their network of trash apartments palaces while coming
up in London's skate scene. Consistent across its advertisements is Palace's humor, the kind found in the all-caps text of
its print ads or in its re-creation of 1980s World Cup matches
to announce Umbro collaborations and a chance to get tossed
over pints with friends and house music. The brand finds comfort in ever bolder stunts, with their pros, for example, riding
horses instead of skateboards to promote a collaboration with
Ralph Lauren.

Palace's full-length skate videos frequently astound skaters worldwide and, if played on mute on a random video wall,
would inspire many to stop and stare. Most notable is *Palasonic*, a full-length offering shot entirely in London on Panaso-
nic M40/M50 VHS camcorders sought out online and hoarded
by Palace's founder and lead lensman, Lev Tanju. Using an aesthetic that would find its way to Instagram filters, Palace developed a signature shot-to-VHS style amid London's terribly

unfriendly streets—full of stones and cracks that Californians accustomed to smooth schoolyards would scoff at. The cameras would frequently malfunction, and tricks would get lost to dysfunctional cameras, forcing both skater and filmer to go back and film difficult, career-defining tricks in streets notoriously poor for skateboarding. The analog style continued in postproduction: After Effects wasn't used in Palace's early videos. As Tanju told *Free Skate Magazine* upon *Palasonic*'s 2018 release, "All the graphics are made from filming off the TV." The result is being able to experience the toy as part of a larger scope of cultures embraced by London's underground.

It's this pursuit and means of capturing the trick that makes skate videos so unique and intrinsically one-shot-takes-all in their approach. It's part of what keeps some of skateboarding's most established filmmakers—some of whom are professionals in the film industry proper—coming back to skateboarding to produce one-off shorts or to digitize their archives to present as historical and educational material for a new generation. Skate videos have survived the fear of their implosion, no matter whether a corporate shoe sponsor is willing to send its team to a ledge in China for a video part. Whether it's footage of a skater on their neighborhood block, a weekend skate trip captured in a short edit, or Palace's video shot over years in London, it's why I keep watching whatever's new, that once-in-a-lifetime accumulation that proves that everyday alchemy is possible.

———

Like many 1990s design strategies for skate brands, the video *Trilogy* by World Industries begins with a DIY rendition of a motion graphic. A homemade version of the 101 logo—which looks like a Green Lantern symbol, with the numbers bunched together—welcomes us to the 101 team's section in this three-team mega-mixtape of a skate video. *Trilogy* is one of the three groundbreaking videos released in 1996, alongside Girl Skateboards' *Mouse* and Toy Machine's *Welcome to Hell*. Like Girl, World's early 1990s videos helped shape street skateboarding's progression and the attitude of '90s schoolyard skating. The Clash's "Death or Glory" plays as the 101 logo rotates, before static distorts the screen and reveals the bootleg operation behind the production: a foam 101 logo, attached to a stick and taped to a turntable. Then the team's four riders are announced by robotic voices at different tempos in the four quadrants of the screen—Clyde Singleton, Marcus McBride, Jason Dill, and Gino Iannucci. The effect is that of a discordant tapestry that, with one's eyes closed, creates a looped-out, trippy vocal trance. Friends and I would sing the different members' names to each other like inside jokes in this weird, independent-film world skateboarding offers.

Maybe it's scenes from this video that pro skater Chad Muska had on his mind when considering his induction into the Skateboarding Hall of Fame in June 2020. At the height of the pandemic and the Black Lives Matter protests centered on the killing of George Floyd, Muska took to social media to tell the skateboarding world that he was not only turning down the nomination but doing so in support of another former pro, a predecessor to Muska, Kareem Campbell.

My mind drifts immediately back to my parents' living room in Southern California, where I watched dubbed VHS copies of both skaters' popular videos: *Fulfill the Dream* by Shorty's Skateboards, featuring Muska, and World Industries' *Trilogy*, featuring Campbell.

A pro rider for World Industries, Campbell was also one of the first pro skaters to own his own company in the 1990s—Menace Skateboards (launched under the World Industries family of brands)—and later founded Axion Footwear, a by-skater, for-skater shoe brand launched with an elite superteam, including Guy Mariano. His pro-model shoe, white with navy and yellow highlights, was so popular that boys and girls who both did and didn't skate were sporting them in junior high. The Menace team had a small montage in *Trilogy*, not a full section of individual parts, but it was soundtracked by "Ain't No N——" from a then relatively unknown Jay-Z. Campbell also had his own individual part in *Trilogy* in the World Industries section.

Muska grew up watching Campbell in early World videos like *Love Child* and *20 Shot Sequence* before Muska reached superstar status in *Fulfill the Dream*. Rising from the ashes of a fractured relationship with his previous sponsor, Toy Machine, Muska was tasked with assembling Shorty's Skateboards' inaugural board team and was featured and introduced to the masses in *Fulfill the Dream* in 1998. Muska was the summer of 1998. His pro-model shoe for éS Footwear had a secret stash pocket inside the tongue, with the first nugs of marijuana I ever saw tucked inside a crushed ziplock peaking out the tongue pocket of a friend's pair. Many non-skaters wore Shorty's hoodies and shirts; one notably had the S on both sleeves. As entrepreneurs and pro riders within the skate industry, Muska and Campbell continued to leverage their popularity into other aspects of popular culture, including becoming characters in the first *Tony Hawk's Pro Skater* video games.

I watched any skate videos in which Muska and Campbell appeared. The living room became a viewing room for all things skateboarding. In addition to turning every curb into melted-dollar-store-candle-wax altars, skateboarding's most disruptive quality was that kids began to commandeer the living room console to obsessively watch skate videos.

What didn't occur to me was that my parents could also hear the unlicensed soul, punk, hip-hop, and beyond soundtracks booming from the living room into their safe space then known as the kitchen table. They initially viewed skateboarding as a materially destructive, potentially cop-attracting activity that I shouldn't be doing.

Over my repetitive plays, I could tell my parents liked the soundtracks of certain videos more than others. I'd try to DJ the situation and create sonic and visual bridges between me and my family through these destined-to-be cult classics. If a New York–specific segment came on, like the 411VM section on Riverside Park or the NYC montage in *Transworld*'s *Interface* and *The Reason*, I'd show my pops, who, despite leaving East Harlem in the early 1970s, could still tell me in what neighborhood and near which major intersection and/or subway stop a given spot was located. My mother employed her knowledge of Los Angeles to call out spots like the Cal State LA ledges in *Goldfish* or the concrete slabs of Inland Empire glory that is Chaffey High School. They helped bolster her stories of taking the bus from La Puente across Los Angeles County just to get to shows and film screenings at UCLA, the LA of her era framed in the passenger windows that I saw anew the moment skateboarding took hold of my sight.

Music is where our bridge really found footing. My parents didn't mind me turning up skate videos with soundtracks plucked from their record collection: soul, salsa, R&B, and 1960s and '70s rock. Sometimes they even told me the artist of the song before I took the time to pause the credits and figure it out. When Jeremy Wray is seen in slow motion grinding a long handrail at the end of Plan B Skateboards' *The Revolution*, it was my folks who immediately recognized the riffs and John Lennon's voice screaming "Alright!" from the Beatles' "Revolution"; they were the ones who knew that Brian Anderson's anti-thought-control soundtrack from *Welcome to Hell* was Pink Floyd. Skate videos like *Mouse* and *Trilogy*, known for their amazing skateboarding and soul soundtracks, were easy hits, as my parents sang along to War's "Magic Mountain," Cymande's "Brothers on the Slide," or Mary J. Blige's "I Love You." They recognized why Spike Jonze used Curtis Mayfield's "(Don't Worry) If There's a Hell Below, We're All Going to Go" to soundtrack his skit, a trailer for the fake blaxploitation film *Brothas from Different Mothas*. They laughed at the inventiveness behind a sketch featuring pro skater Eric Koston in full Charlie Chaplin attire, mimicking what would happen if Chaplin stumbled upon skateboarding in Torrance, California. It sparked conversations with my parents about what Mayfield meant by *the hell below*; the context of his tunes during an era of *Shaft*, Wattstax, Stevie Wonder, and funk; and how the 1970s were really the '60s for many regarding socioeconomic, political, and sexual liberation—and you can hear it in the songs alongside every trick.

———

One afternoon, after watching Kareem Campbell's *Trilogy* part for the third consecutive time, my mom laughed after his slow-motion nollie hardflip over a picnic table. "I like that line," she said. "It's clever."

It took me a moment to realize she was referring to the rap delivered by Nasir Jones, a.k.a. Nas, when he says, "I'd open every cell in Attica / send 'em to Africa." Painting his vision of what a world would look like if Nas were in control, Campbell's part in *Trilogy* enabled my parents to see the socially conscious dimension of hip-hop and how it related to the Last Poets albums they started playing when I turned ten years old, warning of the conditions of Black America's streets.

Part of the reason my parents placed needle to record was the Southern California in which I was raised, a decade that started with the Los Angeles riots, transitioned into the yearslong O. J. trials, and continued with the punitive three-strikes policy of California governor Pete Wilson. Wilson's infamous Proposition 187, which attempted to create a state-administered citizenship system that denied immigrants basic social services, stripping them of health care and access to education, faced public outcry and was ultimately deemed unconstitutional. As predominantly Black and Brown skaters pushed street skateboarding forward at San Francisco's Justin Herman Plaza and the schoolyards of Los Angeles, they were progressing the form under a heightened state of police brutality and incarceration of Black and Brown men throughout California. Tales of the World crew skating Lockwood describe the skaters getting the pass from local gangs affiliated with Fabian Alomar's family, but what of the state-sponsored violence of 1990s Los Angeles?

The decade closed with the infamous Rampart scandal within the Los Angeles Police Department (LAPD), exposing the violent, corrupt anti-gang task force Community Resources Against Street Hoodlums (CRASH) that patrolled Rampart Village and neighboring areas. CRASH framed civilians and gang members alike in gang-related killings, its members committing perjury to double down on their false charges. The scandal resulted in more than one hundred civil cases filed against the LAPD and over $125 million in punitive damages. In 2018, the *Los Angeles Times* broke an investigation about gangs permeating units of the Los Angeles County Sheriff's Department, including a unit with white supremacist ties in Compton, a predominantly and historically Black neighborhood. These units, like CRASH, also have their own identifying tattoos. In 2021, a Loyola Marymount University study "identified 18 such groups that have existed over the last five decades." In May 2023, the county inspector general ordered thirty-five sheriff's deputies to report for a physical examination to see if any had gang-affiliated tattoos. Instead of complying, the officers sued through their union representatives just days after the order.

The extent of the CRASH scandal is immeasurable two decades later, but what is known is that many of CRASH's harmful acts were done in greater Silver Lake, Echo Park, and East Hollywood—the areas of Los Angeles that Kareem Campbell and the World and Girl crews helped put on the map for skate-boarders through their video parts. By *Trilogy*'s release, incarceration rates were increasing in Black communities, not only for three-strikes-related charges but for predominantly nonviolent crimes and drug offenses—despite the concurrent rise of violent crimes within white populations during the same ten-year period from 1985 to 1995, according to a U.S. Department of Justice bulletin.

As such, Campbell and company created and documented some of the most amazing street skateboarding in the culture's history during the most punitive era against Black citizens in Los Angeles by the city's police forces. Campbell's teammate Shiloh Greathouse, who grew up in the neighborhoods near Lockwood Elementary, filmed his *Trilogy* part fresh off a sixteen-month prison bid. His last trick, a backside noseblunt slide across the entire top of a picnic table, was from his first skate session after release. Greathouse filmed and completed his part over the next six months while living in a halfway house. As Nas says at the top of his raps soundtracking Campbell's USC line, "Imagine smoking weed in the streets without cops harassin' / Imagine going to court with no trial." The bars begin with a dream and end with a nightmare portrait of our courts; my folks feared that this new fad, this skateboard thing, would lead me into the streets, toward those forces neither they nor I could control despite the new compass I directed beneath my feet.

My parents knew the stats and the streets, having grown up in Mexico by way of La Puente and in Santurce, Puerto Rico, by way of East Harlem—two hoods on either side of the States—knowing the supposed threat of first impressions kids like me can make on law enforcement, which led to a mix of model-minority expectations and sheer overly hammered common sense, so they ensured that I knew, even before skateboarding, that my privileges were different. With skateboarding, the bleached hair, massive pants, and beyond-PG graphics were antithetical to their goal of keeping me away from trouble. In their eyes, presenting myself as a skateboarder was a visual rebellion and a double-down call for police harassment. Voluntarily wearing a shirt that said AMERICAN ZERO was a privilege I'd never have despite being born in the States. They were warning me about how I was entering the world in general, let alone as a skateboarder: that what I see as innocent, playful fun is, for others, a reason to control the outcome of my life.

Consider Natas Kaupas wearing a Public Enemy shirt while inventing street skateboarding; he inspired many white skaters to be down with hip-hop, to recognize the irony of a skateboarder being labeled a public enemy, to explicitly back Chuck D's burgeoning brainchild, and to implicitly say that Black lives matter. It's not a sponsor's shirt or a graffiti-scrawled statement of their own witty design. It's an alignment with an image and a culture "outside" of skateboarding through the act of skateboarding. The photos, taken by Tod Swank and J. Grant Brittain for Kaupas' 1989 *Transworld* pro spotlight, create the historical documentation and the impact by which we measure the trick. And when it hits magazine pages it shows that not only is Kaupas ripping and innovating across LA's westside schoolyards, but he's also doing so while listening to some of the most bombastic, fist-in-your-face music ever heard.

The specter of illegitimate incarceration and the carceral middlemen between freedom and jail lurk at every session.

When a Brown kid starts skateboarding in any era, they are entering a policed world that presumes their guilt, accelerated now by the four wheels propelling them, sometimes illegally, down city streets, schoolyards, back alleys. We enter society always as the Other and dismantle the systemic racism behind the idea of a skateboarder with every push, every pair of Dickies against dark skin above white wheels and neon wood, every pack of BIPOC kids bombing the streets from spot to spot. Skateboarding is rebellion incarnate, but mobbing spots with a pack of kids that look like you feels closer to the physical reclamation of so-called public space. The excitement and terror fueling this feeling is akin to wearing two Public Enemy shirts, twice the targets on our backs, without the benefit of being a Kaupas in the eyes of the police. I felt the specter of police violence constantly. When kicking us out of spots, cops would separate me from my white friends, asking them how they knew me, if we were from the same town and school.

I think of all this in the wake of a recent email from my mom, checking in and slightly reminiscing about my days growing up skating in the street in front of our house, how I'd yell for her to witness my next handful of attempts, trying to land a new flip trick. Then she delivered an unprompted and belated cautionary tale.

"You have no idea how much I worried about you while you were out skating," she wrote. "But I kept telling myself that I needed to give you the space to make your own mistakes and that whatever we had taught you would somehow surface and allow you to survive."

When my sister moved to college at Berkeley, I visited her by myself when I was thirteen. She kept me on a safe but loose leash, allowing me to explore Telegraph Avenue. Incense smoke tickled my nostrils for the first time as I stared at tables upon tables stacked with the most progressive bumper stickers I'd ever seen. I skated around and found 510 Skateboarding, the now long-standing Bay Area skate shop, at its small original location right on Dwight and Telegraph. The folks behind the counter were super kind, took pity on my board, and even replaced a broken bearing for me free of charge. I bought whatever stickers the contents of my Velcro wallet could afford, knowing even then it was good etiquette. The fact that I found them was probably telling to them, seeing my board and a bunch of SoCal-related stickers, knowing I was an out-of-towner. Toward the back of the store was a living room situation with a TV and a bunch of skate videos, a couch, some chairs. Taped to the top of the TV was a cardboard sign that read THIRTY-MINUTE LURK LIMIT, specifying the time patrons were allowed to lurk at the store and watch skate videos for free before being asked to keep it pushing.

I thought it was so cool there was even a space for locals to watch videos, time limit and all: a theater space within a shop space, all centered around skateboarding and the community it fosters. I forcefully created this theater in my parents' living room as a kid with every VHS I shoved into the VCR, but imagine the walls that could be broken with small amenities like this in every skate shop, the new worlds to be found by kids and parents alike. I remember as a kid staring at that cardboard sign and wishing a space like this would have no lurk limit, no time ceiling for the power of shared experience that skate videos can conjure. But at the very least, it was an invitation to a safe, shared space for skaters.

It reminds me of those spaces highlighted in Kareem Campbell's *Trilogy* part. In a brief interlude sketch, Campbell writes to Shiloh Greathouse in prison. Campbell's desk is covered with malt liquor, cigarettes, joints, and cash. He signs off his letter—"But yo, —you gotta break out and I gotta break out. World for Life. Kareem"—before Lauryn Hill sings the opening melody to "If I Ruled the World (Imagine That)" and Campbell finishes the second half of his part. Through skate videos and the boundaries they break through self-representation, Campbell was right: you gotta break out and I gotta break out from the invisible biases to the literal abusive behavior, those forces threatening to imprison our tricks, stories, letters from ever being received.

5.

WHOSE STREETS?

Skateboarding's intimidation factor is still its most appealing aspect: it is a secret world where culture, fashion, physicality, and self-expression collide. The twenty-first century has been a boom time for skateboarding, which has grown increasingly professionalized, with corporate sponsors and organized competitions such as the X Games and the Olympics influencing it—and in the eyes of some, altering it beyond recognition. And while skate culture is extremely tight-knit, skaters have had to contend with this ever-evolving landscape that is in many ways fundamentally at odds with the purity of the scene, a purity that begins at first love with the board and quickly blooms in the act of skateboarding itself. So as skateboarding becomes increasingly monetized and globalized, while professional skateboarders themselves remain unorganized and stratified, can the purity (or love) remain over the course of a career—or life—spent skateboarding?

My first glimpse of skateboarding was on television, watching skaters fly out of a half-pipe in the skies of Tom Petty's "Free Fallin'" music video. I only knew about skating through its mainstream televised cameos: Breckin Meyer, a.k.a. Travis

Birkenstock, from *Clueless* and his crew of spoiled rebels. The MTV *Real World: Miami* cast member Sarah, who cruised around Florida on a Sector 9 board. ESPN's broadcast of the new X Games competition of action sports, street and vert skateboarding included. And *MTV Sports* featuring the Warped Tour, a punk-and-ska remix of Lollapalooza.

Years later I remembered that a cousin had left her decade-old Price Club skateboard in my garage—a heavy orange-and-black Action Sports Kamikaze board with stiff trucks and oversize black wheels, the board's graphic a knockoff of pro skateboard legend Christian Hosoi's iconic Rising Sun board—and I started pushing it around before the skateboard's trucks quickly fell apart. A truck's hanger connects to the baseplate through a small pivot cup and bushing. It was this bushing that was busted and made the hanger so loose that when any pressure was applied to the tail, lifting the front of the board, the hanger would come loose and spin 180 degrees together with the wheel axle, immediately causing me to slam.

Still, I learned how to ride and cruise the street on this flawed board. At least it forced me to push my weight down as I figured out how to push—front foot on board, back foot pushing. Pushing felt amazing. Skating offered the perspective of a runner, the speed of something close to a bike. The freedom of movement, body fully exposed and legs kicking it forward, allowed me to occupy space differently, boldly. And with a loudness that proclaimed the precariousness of the toy itself. The sound demanded attention while I recognized myself as a projectile. But with this outdated board, I felt little else but fear. I needed something functional and modern and started plotting.

Circa 1996, as skateboarding resurged in popularity, I met skaters at school who were more connected to the local scene than I was, friends of friends sponsored by Utility Board Shop (UBS), the neighborhood skate shop. These skaters were my entry point into the world of more skilled, locally recognized skateboarders, those who received an occasional free deck and an evergreen discount to UBS. I didn't get invited to skate with some of them—instead I befriended those in my existing friend groups who had also started skating—but between these crews I accumulated enough hand-me-down parts that, along with a newly purchased blank bargain board from UBS, I could put together my first proper, complete, modern skateboard. I bought some skateboarding VHS tapes from behind the counter at the skate shop and began watching them, memorizing the movements that define skateboarding's guerrilla film industry. I learned how to ollie—that foundational move of popping the tail and rising with first the front foot and then the back, balancing in a perfect leap midair—and, quickly, how to fall, tumbling rather than extending my wrists to break the impact. Those friends who kept skating became my accomplices every weekend, finding schoolyards and parking lots to learn and practice tricks in. During the week after school, I'd stay sharp by practicing alone on my block or at the nearby basketball court. A regimented obsession developed, and by the beginning of 1997, just after turning twelve, I was hooked.

When I did get my first proper setup, I made the all-too-common error of putting my trucks on backward and felt the uneven pull in the board's direction, not knowing that something was deeply wrong until I pored over skate magazines and realized my mistake. Like many skaters, my sense

of ownership—and my true indoctrination into the sport—
began the moment I physically assembled this first board. To
do it right, you must avoid any number of pitfalls, as I had discovered: bearings unevenly slammed into wheels or air bub-
bles introduced into the grip tape as you go through the act of
"gripping your board"—applying the adhesive, sandpaper-like
black tape to the top of a skateboard deck. Applying grip tape
as you see fit establishes a connection to the board you are creating, curating, and preparing for a lifetime of adventure. You
come to know your board through this ritual act. Gripping the
board is as necessary a skill as ollieing, something you learn
once at a skate shop and do for yourself for the rest of your
skating life—because it's your board and this is what skaters
do. It's as much an identifying rite of passage as the act of riding a board itself.

Skateboarding involves putting your trust in a wooden toy
and going outside, pushing through the streets, and integrating your environment—curbs, ledges, stairs, potholes—into
one more fundamental part of your relationship with the
board beneath your feet. Many skaters don't even use the regulated skateparks designed and legalized for their convenience;
most are poorly designed, built without input from skaters after multiple rounds of city council debates on whether to have
them in the first place. Why skate there when you can take
your board and hit the streets, basking in the temporal ownership you feel as you repurpose underutilized public space,
knowing an unmarked, red-painted curb first grinded by you
and your board is somehow now "yours"?

As in most sports, it's easy to become proficient with a bit
of persistence although exceedingly difficult to go pro.

Still, unlike surfing, where regardless of the size of an ocean's tide, few citizens bat an eye at the sight of surfers paddling in the water, skateboarding on the streets can anger civilians. The sound alone of skaters mobbing down the block is enough to make pedestrians shake their heads in disapproval at what they view as reckless vandalism. But skating belongs in the streets, in a relationship with an environment where skaters can find and accumulate "spots"—public locations not intended for skateboarding that lend themselves to particular, nuanced tricks. These spots are chosen for the creativity their features engender—staircases to descend, handrails to grind or slide, ledges with straight ends for more effortless dismounts. Skaters seek spots wherever they go, and once they find them, they calculate whether to take the concomitant risks: tickets from cops, physical injury, even getting hit by a car if the landing of a spot is in a busy place. They also learn the unspoken rules of ownership as they frequent these spots, weighing the balance of foot traffic and the possible presence of law enforcement against ample opportunities to execute an intended trick. If a spot is central, like a city hall or courthouse steps, skaters will schedule their sessions against the tide of civilians' routines in urban spaces. These aren't turf battles, as you might see in surfing, due to a kind of etiquette. If you're sponsored, don't repeat a legendary trick in the same legendary spot. Don't blow up the spot by littering or graffitiing nearby businesses. One could call this "owning" the spot, but many skaters know such ownership is brief.

This dynamic relationship with public space speaks to what skaters always own: the knowledge that unless you fully submit to the act of skateboarding itself, you will never truly understand the culture—let alone the cockiness and confidence acquired when falling becomes an option, however controllable, with scabs on elbows like encrusted merit badges earned by trying to learn something new. This new thing often seemed unachievable mere days earlier—an idea that is transformed into a physical, accomplished act. When you land a trick after hours of trying, you feel not so much a celebration but an exhalation, a release of relief. The skill and humility involved in learning to skate create a velvet rope between skater and civilian that lies glamorously across schoolyards, back alleys, and downtown ledges, welcoming anyone and daring them to enter.

Even though municipalities attempt to constrain skateboarding with statutes and laws, the sport itself is completely unregulated. With the exception of skateboarding competitions like in the Olympics, there are no rules and no referees. There is no time limit or predetermined selection of performed tricks, let alone a shot/serve/pitch clock. There's no governing body regulating COVID protocol. There are no coaches and no prescribed goals other than to progress individually in the act of skateboarding itself.

Indeed, with so few rules and so little structure, this vague idea of what it means to be a skater—someone who takes comfort in the solitary endeavor, who shares in a world view that embraces the possibilities and perils that pursuing this activity can manifest—may be the one thing holding us skaters together. It's fitting that in a sport inherently imbued with—and dominated by—risk, skaters are comfortable with this arrangement. What's ironic is that as skate culture has traditionally rejected rules and conventions, high-profile contest skaters competing on television and featured in video games now increasingly rely on corporate structures to execute their professional skateboarding. Pro skating is, in a sense, an opportunistic caste system, with a top tier of current or legacy pros making solid money by way of contest circuits such as Street League Skateboarding, Vans Park Series, and the Olympics and wide-ranging corporate endorsements (even Weedmaps briefly had a skate team).

Whatever cohabitation exists between skater and corporate sponsor, skater and city, skater and citizen, or skater and urban developer, skaters have the power to be alchemists anywhere. It's truly electric that the path of least resistance is often the way street skateboarding finds its place in the world. Part of the power of stepping on a board is feeling like a conduit to an energy loop of skater, board, and movement through space. And to make our sport more progressive is to acknowledge how much we are part of larger movements changing all spaces, skate spots and parks included, and their new identities.

Maybe we're just efficient survivalists. Dedicated urban parasites turned sponsored craftspeople. If there's anything skaters own more than the streets, it's knowing when collective action is necessary. We recognize that as a group we can help save public spaces from forces of gentrification, as when the Lower Manhattan crew powered by the website Quartersnacks prevented the Astroturfing of the legendary Tompkins Square Park in the East Village, one of the few paved park spaces left for skaters and pedestrians alike. The efforts of the Long Live Southbank coalition of London skaters not only preserved but remodeled and expanded the undercroft that gave birth to British street skating so that all could enjoy it. Recognizing this influential role in our communities, we've stepped up to have conversations and raise awareness around issues like gender-based violence, sexual consent, suicide prevention, and LGBTQIA+ rights.

I'm glad I can even say these things now, as a skater, without hesitation. It's nice to see more joy and less cool. People are attracted to skateboarding and its culture because of the love and creativity skateboarders have injected into our communities, knowing this is something worth falling for, a chance to be a part of its possibility.

6.

PUBLIC DEMONSTRATION

At the top of the ten-stair, I asked my cousin Alex for the strength to fully commit—to propel my body across and down and smoothly beyond the double-digit barrier between decent and good skateboarder—and ollie the massive ten-stair leading into our junior high school's quad, regardless of the physical consequences. This is for Alex. Do it for Alex. I imagined his reply from a cloud next to our abuela somewhere in the sky looking west toward Rose Hills off the 605 where they both rest, nodding their approval with a shrug. His glasses still on, his Danzig-ish hairdo encased in its 1993 existence. Four years after his death I wondered if he'd be proud of me, for finding a path that led me to skateboarding, its culture, to believing my body could be this odd sum of parts maneuvering ideas into ridiculous actions. For changing my trajectory whether I could see it or not. But I felt Alex could, and I needed our private chat to guide my public commitment to spiritual and physical alignment for a trick. My actual literal form was changing daily within my corduroy cargos, Emerica blue canvas sneakers, and crew-neck black sweatshirt, puberty progressing through my almost-thirteen-year-old frame.

But here, on a daunting set of stairs, some spiritual call felt necessary. A Saturday morning was no longer dedicated to cartoons but to creativity and bloodshed, and this day, the anniversary of the parental union engendering my existence, I had insisted on a sleepover at E's house the night before, so we could wake up and head straight to our school for a quick session before skating to neighboring San Dimas to attend my first skate demo. Pros, ams, stickers, ramps—the skate industry was in town for an afternoon, and we had to bear witness. E was always down for a mission and a night of psychological preparation obsessing and rewinding VHS skate videos and eating probably burgers from the In-N-Out up the street. Maybe an attempt to watch scrambled pornography on the Playboy Channel.

I wasn't religious. Prayer for me was rare and uttered out of desperation more so than faith. Still, local churches held community sway, with many of my classmates' weekends occupied by various church activities. At the time, these churches were trying to connect being a skater with being a believer, and my small prayer reminded me of the only time I'd ever attended a Bible study.

E was there too. He'd told me about this church downtown that'd let kids skate if you stayed for a weird communal prayer session that somehow involved songs. The trick was showing up early to help set up ramps, testing them out, so to speak, and then bailing before you had to worship something, or someone, you didn't believe in. It was two quarter pipes against a wall, allowing kids to drop in and skate a couple boxes, maybe a jump ramp. It was nothing, really, but it was one of the few pop-up skateparks of its kind that actually lasted a good amount of time without a neighbor complaining or a cop kicking us out, something over which we kids had a modicum of control.

Skateparks were highly liable, private affairs that weren't prevalent in our area, other than the BMX-designed "skatepark" called the Edge at the Irwindale Expressway along the 605. The church would stamp skaters' hands during the skate sessions and refuse entry to the parking lot ramps after service without this hand-stamped proof of prayer. It's like they wanted us to learn how to smudge bullshit devices of verification into existence, and so we learned.

E was good, could drop in on the tallest ramp, and basically had the spot dialed by the time the local churchgoing kids showed up. Their boards were fairly pristine, and they were mostly beginners, jumping on this new skateboarding trend thing, giving it a go through the local house of God. E and I kept skating as some mutual friends showed up, but as the sun went down, the Bible group got closer; I'd fake a fall and go behind the wall on the other side of the ramps and make a dash for it. Other times I'd simply walk away when the elders weren't looking. But sometimes I'd forget the time, lose myself in the actual joy of skating ramps for a change, look up, and find E already gone.

A friend and I got stuck, gave in, and went to a prayer session. I couldn't tell if my friend was serious about it or was familiar enough with churches to code switch, socially pass. The pastors spoke about the space afforded by the church—the ramps and the parking lot and sometimes pizza for those who stayed for youth group service. The guilt trip was a psychological bear trap for juveniles. I was jealous E had snuck off before getting reeled into the church. He was probably already drinking or smoking at the Circle K patio benches down the street, out of earshot of those songs we sang in a church as old as this town when it was named Lordsburg, and despite our differences, neither E nor I got closer to God those nights but tried skating something new. A variety of spots and obstacles to skate fuels a skater's creativity and skills. With few skateparks at the time, and street spots hit-or-miss depending on security, missions like this, even when playing cat and mouse with the church, felt necessary to keep that creative spark going.

Years later, it's still insulting: to use skateboarding as the carrot and a parking space's legality to lure skaters for a few dumb hours into a faux community centered around free pizza and not getting kicked out. A skateboard is a toy, not a lure, let alone one dangled from a cross. Still, there were brands during this time like Renaissance Skateboards that had scripture quotes and biblical references in their ads. Similarly, upturn the soda cups we grew up drinking out of from In-N-Out and find a scripture quote. The intersection of conservative culture and its attempts to co-opt alternative lifestyles seemed a particularly Southern Californian affair, where preachers, doomsayers, and more collided, awaiting Judgment Day.

That morning with E, I feared that ten-stair was my Judgment Day incarnate, ten portals of brimstone to experience upon each attempt. Alex's reply was nowhere that morning when I spoke directly to him, but his spirit was everywhere, pushing hesitation aside and becoming my blood, a buzzing I felt when mind, body, and stupidity collided for a trick I'd never executed before, with my skateboard and flesh at least. I had a Maple Skateboards deck that was so wide and heavy

CHIPPED   69

it felt like driving a boat across sand dunes. The runway was part of an angled cul-de-sac of buildings, like the arm of an upside-down *U*, and I stretched my arms above my head, breathing and feeling the haze evaporate with the sun's arrival. I ran on my board and pushed hard. I bent and ollied as far as I could. That feeling of flight I've never experienced again. Halfway down I felt my legs ready to accept a fortunate fate, to land on the board and let me cleanly ride away, ready for the impact, amazed at this new feeling of an additional two stairs to clear, those pages of psychological barriers flipped open like magazines in the wind. I landed bolts but my body fell forward, overcompensating for my weight, and I safely tumbled across the landing while my board remained in place. "I did it, Alex," I said. "I committed." I was terrified of trying it again; I was just getting familiar with the already rite-of-passage eight-stair around the corner, only able to ollie it, let alone do the huge backside kickflips local legends could execute at leisure. I gave up, felt good with my land-to-slam, didn't want to get hurt. Maybe I wanted to film it for whatever burgeoning skate video project we were gestating in seventh grade. Maybe I knew I would sprain my knee on this same set doing a weaker attempt a few months later, putting me in crutches for a few weeks and soreness the rest of my life. But we needed to get to Active Ride Shop in San Dimas. We needed to see skateboarding.

Most know the town of San Dimas from the movie *Bill & Ted's Excellent Adventure*, based in and shot on location at San

Dimas High School, a five-minute skate from the skate shop.
A few years after this demo, the band the Ataris would make
their name with the song "San Dimas High School Football
Rules," a quote from *Bill & Ted's*. When we drove by the Circle K near the town's library, we always wondered if, indeed,
George Carlin had touched down via time-traveling pay phone
and silver trench coat, teaching Gen X about world history,
babes, and rock 'n' roll. Those scenes were actually shot in
Tempe, Arizona, but we always thought, How couldn't this
film be made here, a suburb designed after other suburbs,
where gold ribbons for soldiers fighting in the Persian Gulf
were tied around the trees along main boulevards?

Two rows of parking spaces in the parking lot of Active
Ride Shop—neighbor to local legend Michaelangelo's Pizza, a
future employer for many friends—were blocked off right at
the entrance to San Dimas off the 57 freeway's terminus at the
210. The shopping center was on brand with the town's larger
western motif, with old wood buildings and wood-planked
sidewalks but also the modern amenities of a Denny's, a
Motel 6, and across the street, Warehouse Music, where we'd
line up for Ticketmaster bracelets to buy Ticketmaster tickets,
camping out all day. A nearby coffee shop where older goths
hosted open mics was where I subsequently read my first poem
in public.

The sound of ramps got louder the closer E and I got to
the demo. The spectacle felt like a welcoming committee for
a spaceship landing, with skaters from the future showing off
their abilities from galaxies beyond. Here I felt the amazement
of aligning entire days for the opportunity to bear witness, to
see possibility turned into real life via effort, creativity in real

time, an improvisation, a calculation, a parking lot taped off with the knowledge that kids would arrive.

Here the boundaries were defined, the parking lot was ours for once, and the level of skateboarding was intense to witness. It was the first time I'd seen somebody do flip tricks into grinds, like local pro JP Jadeed's kickflip noseslide or Chet Thomas's hardflip backside 50-50, both down the small hubba ledge. Mike York was trying to get enough pop from a small kicker ramp to kickflip into a frontside noseslide on a box turned on its short side, making it taller and that much more difficult. One of the progenitors of street skateboarding, Mike Vallely, hand planted the big bank near where we were standing, while wearing Airwalk shoes. He had a signature lightning bolt board graphic from either his second (or third?) stint on Powell or his soon-to-be-launched Transit Skateboards, one of many board brands he'd helm between contracts with larger companies like Element. He was kind enough to interrupt his session and sign whatever paper or stickers we had for him to scrawl across in Sharpie. Tim Brauch was also nearby, ollieing from the big bank over the crowd barricade and into the street near Michaelangelo's. He was the coolest of the bunch, asking us how we were doing while signing our crap. Months later his *Transworld Skateboarding* poster, timed to coincide with his feature interview, would be on most of our walls, despite him riding for Santa Cruz and us growing up in Southern California, and months after that he'd pass away from a brain aneurysm. I think a young James Craig and mysterious Orange County legend Ronnie Creager were also in attendance, but here my memory fades. If a photographer or videographer was there that day I can't remember, and maybe no one else can either without some type of historical record. But I was there, thankfully.

I hoped my parents would understand my not spending the entire day with them, the need to sleep over and hurl myself down stairs before seeing abilities beyond my comprehension turn a ten-stair into child's play with these skaters' tech-meets-hesh, flip-into-grinds-down-ledges wizardry. And I think of Alex and the stories of him hanging around the Upland Pipeline before it closed, and how long he'll wait for me to make my trick, if I'll curse his name for being gone or praise him again for the courage to try. I wanted to come home and show my parents something they fought so hard to find as kids and only discovered it reluctantly as a bruised peach. I wanted to show them a realized joy.

───────

I asked permission again for a longer road trip with E and his mom down into Orange County to Huntington Beach's small but historic skatepark directly next to the high school on Beach Boulevard. They had this old 1980s caramel-tan Mercedes that felt luxurious compared to our over-upholstered Oldsmobile. E's mom was kind of a babe, the kind of SoCal woman for whom Tom Petty songs were written and whom beach culture was designed to spotlight. *Wayne's World 2* was filmed near their home, the caricature-driven scene of the wise, naked Native American man giving water to a shirt-and-jeans-clad Mike Myers along D Street next to Bonita High School. During shoot breaks, E's mom got a photo with Mike Myers but not the nearly nude man. That happened in 1993, the same year Alex passed and a summer whose songs, TV shows, cars, and more are ingrained in my mind.

E's mom drove us first to a particular OC Circuit City store that had discounts on tape-to-tape editing kits. E's skateboarding was that good as to necessitate a home-film department for a sponsor-me tape. Or maybe it was for bootlegging skate videos into mixtapes (that I would hopefully receive). The benefits were boundless. His parents built miniramps in his backyard and he always had a pro-model board, twenty dollars more than the shop boards I rode. E and his mother had a funny, combative relationship, bickering like a married couple one moment, E being sweet to his mom the next. It was a peek into white culture, with fewer lines of age established between the two generations. Something new and different.

Orange County was Disneyland, the 57 freeway, my mom's alma mater at Cal State Fullerton, and the chess league I briefly attended somewhere near Buena Park. Huntington Beach was a new side of suburbia, one cut from a similarly conservative postwar cloth as the citrus-to-suburb Inland Empire but different from the communities of the greater San Gabriel Valley, a mix of Latinos pushed out of East Los Angeles and like-minded Southeast Asian, Black, Korean, Persian, and Indian communities. And white folks too: working-class veterans and former coast guards and contractors and cops and teachers alike. The sprawl above the 60 held a culture different than that of Surf City, USA. Growing up, you hear rumors about skinheads at the pier, briefly reported incidents of potential hate crimes. Of hardcore and punk scenes marred by violence.

The cop station is across the street from the small kidney of a skatepark, which is next to Huntington Beach High School.

This is where Ed Templeton, Jason Lee, Mike Vallely, Jason Dill, and Mark Gonzales helped shape and define street style in the late 1980s and early '90s. In addition to the nearby pay 'n' play courts' ramp jams, the high school is where initial grinds and slides on handrails were perfected, where Templeton did early ollie impossibles down stairs, and where freestylers like Don Brown knew their career's end was near (and into business ownership he and others went).

Templeton's generation gave way to stuntmen like La Habra's Jeremy and Jonas Wray and Liverpool import turned OC ripper Tom Penny, ripping a backside tailslide up the short hubba ledges to fakie, landing at the top of the stairs so casually his khaki chinos and gray sneakers and shoes looked undisturbed by the grass, waxed concrete, and dirt surrounding him, setting the scene for his potential failures. His kickflip backside 50-50 and kickflip backside tailslides were executed perfectly in the back of the school on benches so waxed they were black slabs of former white concrete, generations of candles melted by the sun and grinded into iconography. These were the spots coveted and showcased in the VHS videos E's new machine would duplicate for eternity, the individualized, crowdsourced archive of skateboarding also rooted in vandalism.

It was also the most likely campus for cops to trap skaters and write tickets. A militarized state, this Orange County. Kid or adult, tickets were dealt just the same. Boards taken and impounded somewhere at an unknown county building or precinct. This was more likely to happen the deeper into the campus skaters went. We continued our tour, passing the four up, four down that Jeremy Wray destroyed in Plan B's

immortal *Second Hand Smoke* video, released just before I
started skating and introduced to me by E. Then the handrail
over which a neophyte of an amateur skateboarder, Andrew
Reynolds, executed a varial heelflip captured by then *Transworld* photographer Atiba Jefferson. And the smaller staircases
that Templeton killed in the early 1990s to the chunky, uber-
waxed benches that Penny and others annihilated, which are
so perfectly tempting to skate, toward the back of the school—
that's where and when the cops arrive, trapping you at the
nearby double-tall fences.

At least that's what E and I heard when we returned to the
skatepark after a brief, cautiously executed cruise through the
school: that a couple of kids got tickets at the benches after us,
at least a hundred dollars. The rumor spread through the small
park frequently described as an ashtray, with its slight, two-
tier format, with a flat bar and two cement benches surrounding a mellow pyramid that, unlike many of the era, looked fun
and accessible to skate. We came back to more kids crowding
the Saturday session, kids like us from outside Orange County
wearing shirts from their local skate shops, unofficial ambas-
sadors of an entire suburb's style and etiquette. I saw my first
noseblunt slide in person and understood why they squealed
so loud on film.

And then this one bro of a skater, seemingly a converted
football running back turned exiled surfer, like the jock cousin
of Sublime's Bradley Nowell, barged into the crowded park either shirtless or wearing a white tee, light-blue denim shorts,
pulled-up tube socks. Everything looked crispy and brand-
new beneath his feet. And he was furious. He was not able
to land whatever tricks he was flinging across the pyramid,

attempts so gaudy they almost mocked the humble obstacle he was unsuccessfully hucking himself over. There was a waist-high retaining wall encircling the park that looked possible to ollie over, but not without a good amount of speed and people getting out of the way. A mother was sitting in a beach chair nearby, watching her young kid figure out the session and unspoken vibes. The grown shirtless skater vaulted an ollie over the wall, very close to the mother, enough wall for him to go wherever he pleased but he chose that specific spot to tell her to leave, to be an asshole, mostly, and unfortunately a skater—and he still didn't land the trick. He soon became one of many blurs in a park filling up with skaters. Before I had time to think about anything, I had to move out of the way of the next skater trying their trick, thinking of Alex back at the Pipeline and if he ever saw worse, both of us knowing the evergreen potential of men at their most empowered.

That was the first day I met a skater I really didn't like, shirtless and skating that old, now-demolished skatepark next to Huntington Beach High School. The cop station remains. His attitude sucked; he was a force rather than a coconspirator or fellow skater, fraternity nonexistent among us fawns, apparently trying to get in where we weren't supposed to fit in, weekender bridge-and-tunnelers of suburbia we were to this scene, Surf City, USA.

The narrative that high school is a divisive petri dish of jocks and nerds couldn't have been more crudely displayed than in me and E. I feel like we stopped talking to each other when we got to high school, or he stopped talking to me. He hung out with cool kids, made it with cool girls, I think graduated but definitely joined the military and served overseas. When in town, I pass by his house and see the part of his parents' backyard visible from the main road and imagine the miniramp standing there overlooking a nearby wash and the kindergarten we all attended, before I pass E's (old?) block and the high school appears to my right. For those four years of high school I kept skating, started garage bands, and read more books. I started writing poems. And soon I begged my parents for rides to shows in Orange County but also Hollywood and the all-ages hometown gem, the Glass House. I wonder if he kept his old boards. His old videos. If he ever made an edit with whatever footage we shot of him doing tricks probably worthy enough for skate-shop sponsorship. If the footage I shot of him is on a Hi8 tape somewhere and if the footage of me doing an ollie down a big eight-stair was even shot. It's weird to see someone so talented in this anti-authority arena of skateboarding voluntarily join that very authority as a lifestyle. As a job. The Marines briefly advertised in *Transworld Skateboarding* and *Thrasher*. I doubt it swayed him either way.

7.

CURBS

Slappies were out of style when I started skating; it was all about pop in 1996. *How many boards can you ollie?* was a normal question asked at spots, running into other skaters, kids eager to judge you according to your pop's potential.

Ollies are foundational to skateboarding. Watching a group of young skaters learn how to ollie is like watching newborn birds flap their wings to learn how to fly, only it's kids using their feet to smack the tails of boards bigger than them, configuring the balance they need to bend their knees, pop the tail with their back foot, and coordinate with the front foot, which turns slightly on its side, kisses the board's grip tape, and raises board and body into that "jump," that lifting off the ground from which all other tricks are made.

Many skaters note the style differences of a high ollie done at speed and a slow stationary ollie with greater board control. Skate-industry trade shows hosted high-ollie changes featuring the vertical abilities of Danny Wainwright or Reese Forbes, who would literally try to ollie from flatground over an increasingly taller limbo stick with measuring tape on its side. Jeremy Wray's pop was incredible. Quim Cardona had his ollies arise from a dance-hall speaker box somewhere in Jamaica, Queens, his legs bent and squatting nearly to the ground before they helped propel Cardona's big ollies over whatever New York's streets had to offer, losing neither rhythm nor riddim in his pop.

But I always wanted to ollie like Kien "Donger" Lieu. He had a massive French braid of a ponytail that thickly hung well below his waist, guiding our eyes toward his striped Pumas before he popped an ollie so high and smooth the viewer forgot he had just cleared a taller-size trash can or fire hydrant from flat. Still photos of him in skate mags showed his knees almost hitting his chin, his ollies were that tucked, hovering over whatever he was clearing with speed upon landing. The astronomical levels of pop in his Maple Skateboards video parts were excerpted in a brief *MTV Sports* profile, showing a day in his life as one of the prominent pros out of the Mission Beach, San Diego, scene. He even wrote poetry and had chapbooks for kids at demos.

Growing up playing basketball, wanting pop wasn't new to me. Dudes came to practice with ankle weights on, official or homespun, before we started circling those weird, duck-looking Strength Shoes, with a front platform underneath the toes, in Eastbay shoe catalogs. All to make you jump higher for dunking and blocking shots. Being tall doesn't help much in skateboarding though, other than having longer legs. If anything, looking down a set of stairs from a taller height increases the fear factor. Still, I had the advantage of long legs, occupying the tall-kid spot in the back row of all school photos since first grade and manifesting my pop before I even knew I'd be trying to part my hair down the middle one day. At the start of sixth grade, I started combing my hair that way because that's what skaters did. I baby-stepped into the culture through mall stores instead of proper skate shops and pleaded with my parents for a pair of Airwalks from a Journeys in the Montclair Mall. It felt crucial to complete my projected skater look before I had any proficiency skateboarding. Fake it till you make it, and I wasn't alone. That first week of school, I noticed a bunch of kids who didn't skate wearing shoes and shirts reminiscent of the cool, actual skaters. Skate culture was crossing over into the mainstream slowly through footwear (like Simple Shoes' and Vans' big-box-store presence) and connected skating with a California lifestyle increasingly exported through MTV.

In an episode of Jeff Grosso's *Loveletters to Skateboarding*, pro skater and Rockridge local Barker Barrett described curbs as "the first problem you encounter on a skateboard. If you rode off one, you had to ride back up one at some point."

When I learned how to cruise and ollie around a bit, I couldn't ollie and land straight, turning ninety degrees and naturally leaning toward my right-hand side. Cruising around my block was stop-and-go as a result, always losing my speed and skirting myself back straight.

I learned how to do it through the tough love of my classmate Ryan and his crew in Covina. They were a gang of kids who all lived in an apartment complex off the 10 freeway near the Eastland Mall, Covina just next door to Pomona. They waxed every curb in that parking lot, it seemed, doing circles while directing traffic, with neighbors' parents coming and going in real Southern Californian time: in cars.

Ryan was the first kid who saw me skate, broke me out of my captivity, and corrected my wrongs. Here's how to stay straight when doing an ollie. Here's how to push without

losing speed. How to recognize that shoulders have as much
to do with landing a trick as your knees and legs. Ryan was a
short soccer player by childhood trade, demonstrated in his
propensity to wear Adidas's early attempts at skateboarding
footwear and in the nimble flick of his kickflips. His hair had
a side part with a wave, the kind of boyhood cut I was trying
to avoid, but he had cool Diadora polo shirts, that European
futból aesthetic turned SoCal skater that I wanted to embody
on sight. Over the weekends, he'd lead me around his spots in
Covina, like the nearby Eastland Mall and all the neighborhood nooks and crannies and gaps and curb cuts along the
way, testing my ability to keep up by keeping my ollies, and
thus speed, straight and fast, trial by fire at not getting lost
and keeping up. Sometimes we'd visit the short-lived Unique
Skateshop on Rowland Avenue and stare at magazines and
videos, pros and amateurs hopping over picnic tables in Los
Angeles or Jersey barriers in Manhattan or across street gaps
in brick-walled Philadelphia—not a slappy in sight. Pop was
the fuel that wanted us to go higher, farther, taller. The goal
was to elevate to higher ledges: the legendary Chaffey High
School ledges in Ontario or the lesser-known but locally classic
ledges at Baldwin Park High School—these were the proving
grounds for shop-sponsored skaters trying to film sponsor-me
tapes for proper skate companies, trying to live the dream of
skating for a living. We didn't know that most of the pros sold
the free product they received to make rent; however more
affordable the 1990s were for some, the hustle of an athlete-
meets-contractor lifestyle remained.

As I got better and skated with Ryan most weekends, I
learned he was the ringleader of a bunch of local skater kids

that all lived in the apartments nearby. We'd leave his apartment parking lot a dozen deep, cutting and cruising our way on those side streets that locals drive along the 10 freeway to avoid getting off at certain annoying exits. I started mapping the path push by push, knowing which planters were empty of trees or stumps, measuring my speed against the kid ahead for a try at an ollie over the planter. If I hung up—my back trucks' kingpin clipping against the lip of the landing and falling short of the required distance to clear—I had to take the hit of the fall while tumbling out of the way in case a kid behind me was trying their ollie (to imminent doom) just the same.

We moved like some juvenile-propelled centipede that can't help but cannibalize itself. We skated to that annoying freeway exit—Barranca—and debated whether the rumor of a known pro skater landing a boardslide on the massive triple-kinked handrail on the corner ever happened. We'd skate either the Eastland Mall's parking lot or the Bank of America seven-stair that occasionally showed up in skate magazines, or we'd do what everyone else around us was doing: going to In-N-Out. DIY lemonades consisted of free water cups, sugar packets, and those complimentary lemons at the soda fountain. One full water cup with this drink was cut across the other smaller water cups the employees smartly gave us, knowing a cup to us was a functional pitcher. Citrus sugar water in tow, we'd head up the hill to South Hills High School, a massive outdoor campus more than a school, almost a small junior college. It had everything we needed: wide-open and covered spaces for flatground, stairs of all sizes, waxed curbs of different heights, small handrails. When the sun started going down, we bombed the hill down Barranca at full speed back through our original route, all the way to our apartment-complex starting point. Years later, I wonder if anyone from that crew, my first crew of skaters, still skates and if they'd be surprised that, out of all of us, the kid that used to ollie crooked up curbs stuck with it.

———

Nobody and everybody was supposed to be here. The subway parking lot had become a neighborhood United Nations used for all outdoor activity. The curbs were used for smoke breaks, coffee meetups, yard sales, and all-day parking. Nobody was going to work because work existed now, for most in this neighborhood, in their homes. Increasingly expensive homes. Sanctuary, residence, office, isolation chamber—home was a leash as much as a destination. *The New York Times* described this pandemic feeling as languishing, and I could relate. The pandemic wore on me. Fortunately, I kept my contract job through the 2020 summer. My contract job turned fully remote, and the length of my sanity shortened with each paranoid day—a release felt imminent. But then like for so many: no work. Halted. Furloughed. Immediate government assistance. A pandemic. The first three months reconfigured everyone's relationship to outside, to the streets. Whether it was denial or the possibility found in navigating ghost towns on foot, space changed and so did the places we called home. Economy, opportunity, and disease collided to force things apart, a collapse of societal function and safety nets that evaporated like the bootstraps they always rested upon.

But at this BART parking lot, a different magic happened, one skaters manifested in their minds since this lot became a street spot back in the 1980s. Abracadabra, and somehow all the parking blocks near the far end started disappearing, allowing more and more waxed curbs to appear on those long islands of concrete divided by the beams supporting the 24 to 980 expressway into downtown Oakland or the Bay Bridge to San Francisco.

Our world of commuting daily to and from San Francisco for work became instead a five-mile radius of socially distanced, double-masked survival in a part of town known for small shops, single-family homes, and historical redlining. Not necessarily the type of demilitarized zone where skateboarding can thrive. But so be it. Even living next to such a historic spot, seen from footage from the 1980s to the present, I was hesitant to skate downtown or even in skateparks. I skated as early as I could to reluctantly avoid as many skaters as possible, not just for access to the spot but because of the fucking pandemic. Infection outside was low but still possible.

The economy plummeted to new lows, stocks and investment portfolios bottom-feeding just the same. Nationwide, small-business revenue was down 20 percent in the first nine months of 2020. There was a genuine fear of skate shops closing, leading to skaters offering mutual aid through their buying power and online skills, with some offering to create the web pages and e-stores for shops struggling to do pickup orders. I bought a new complete board from my local. It was handed to me outside, fully set up and wrapped in plastic, by a masked employee thanking me for the support. It was funny figuring out how close either of us would get, this awkward game of chicken played in the early stages of the pandemic.

The deck was by Unity, one of the first queer skate

companies based in Oakland and soon to be distributed by Deluxe Distribution in San Francisco, a cornerstone of the industry and a testament to the brand's reach. Unity is more collective than team, and the Rockridge Curbs was one of their local spots. Many members of their crew were featured in a *New York Times* Styles-section photo gallery, some in long peacoats doing a synchronized duet of slappy nosegrinds, perfectly tweaked just slightly over the curb, for an instant classic of a secular, non-skate-magazine editorial photo.

Here was my physical and metaphorical break from my 1990s roots: With this board I will do slappies all day, not caring about what's broken or what doesn't look aesthetically correct; the act will dictate the look, and everything will follow. This board will be the most destroyed board I'll ever have. And like this board, I too will change. It wasn't just the pandemic that made me feel stuck in the mud; that mud was adulthood, and I'd let it take priority. I was leading a professional and artistic life inspired by skateboarding but not rooted in the lessons gleaned from staying connected to the act itself. I had nothing to look forward to, no desire to learn anything new but merely to stay proficient at a handful of tricks that made me feel relevant as a skater, like a kickflip on flatground. Slappies gave me a goal and a challenge. I'd skate around the nearby Safeway parking lot at night, refamiliarizing myself with the limits of my skate abilities in the near darkness, otherwise alone. Deer from Temescal Creek strolled through the back of the parking lot, rustling near the trees between my fledgling attempts at making my left knee feel strong again before figuring out slappies at the Rockridge BART.

The irony is that slappies were created not too far from

those Covina and Pomona streets where I learned how to skate, a little closer to downtown Los Angeles in Whittier. This is where John Lucero architected the slappy, when Lucero was bored in the parking lot of Whittier Skatepark in the mid-to-late 1980s. Kicked out of the skatepark, a.k.a. Skate City, with friend Richard Armijo for being, in Lucero's words, "total idiots," he started sessioning the curbs out front instead, banging into them and emulating the ramps he wanted to be skating inside the park. Whether the right angle of a curb or the small pyramid-top, scaled edges of a parking block for cars, Lucero explored these new dimensions with speed, creating and helping to popularize slappies right there in that parking lot.

Unlike an ollie into the grind, a slappy is when you approach a curb at velocity and bash the trucks into a grind without an ollie. The front truck is bashed first before the back truck follows, the grind executed by muscling into position rather than popping in. Slappies destroy your trucks, grinding away at the axles and loosening the kingpins in new ways after they're slammed repeatedly into curbs, daring the trucks to grind as fast as possible in whatever position the body suggests. Lucero's boredom unintentionally generated a new component to street skating. In the Bay Area, I associate slappies with the Safeway curbs in San Francisco off Church and Duboce, where Danny Sargent and Tommy Guerrero and countless others turned that small stretch into their proving ground.

Learning slappies meant overcoming the internalized judgments that came with skateboarding in the 1990s. Fuck how many boards I could ollie or whether slappies were outdated tricks in the eyes of those '90s pros whose interviews and opinions about skateboarding shaped my own. This was a reclamation of possibility. Of reconfiguring my feet to move with my hips and torque my body into a slappy. I thought about older skate photos, like Hugh Holland's from the 1970s of skaters on short banana boards pushing along the banks of a schoolyard in the valley or those videos from the 1980s showcasing first-generation street skaters Eric Dressen and Tom Knox. Lucero himself was emulating '70s skaters slashing the coping at the lips of swimming pools. His canvas was simply a parking block, killing time amid skatepark detention.

I developed a pandemic-meets-unemployment skating routine—Monday mornings, Thursdays or Fridays, maybe a weekend, and repeat—that avoided crowds as much as preserved pride. Sweating and doing "laps" around the spot is something new for an old act, with a goal not of exorcizing dead past selves and former abilities but of exploring the living present turned future with every push.

No matter the age, being a skateboarder lends itself to caustic stares from passersby, from those believing that any noncommercial activity in an underutilized parking structure will diminish their property values. There's a small home near the curbs that has a miniature gnome home in its front lawn, something of a local attraction for the attentive shoegazer. It is that small. When I skated past it to the curbs, I wondered if it's some public-installation commentary on the inequitable distribution of single-family homes in the Bay Area, on investment firms buying up as many homes as citizens, driving up prices as a result.

There was this carousel of morning characters who used the lot for their own purposes. There was a woman in her fifties who parked one car before walking across the lot to another and driving away—same two cars, every day. Parents teaching their kids how to ride bikes like their parents assumedly did, but this time in medical masks and with hand sanitizer at the ready. The fedora-adorned, artisan-presenting gentleman getting a shot of espresso from the corner, giving me a wave. The woman in yoga pants who couldn't help but walk diagonally across the spot, midsession, demanding that the tricycling toddlers and too-grown skaters stop in her presence. The random gentleman so covered up in a black face mask and painter's gear that he looked like Antifa infantry, ready to fight fascists infiltrating UC Berkeley. Instead, he was using a mobile hose to paint the freeway's support pillars white again.

My favorite might have been the opportunistic capitalists, the pop-up, cool-kid streetwear shops, cutting out the middleman and going straight to consumer—parent sponsored and all. Kids sold streetwear out the trunks of their parents' minivans. Skaters and LARPers had used the space the longest, but now everyone was finding their opportunity as the pandemic continued.

The popularization of the curbs broke through the NIMBYism and historical redlining of Rockridge by refuting the idea that a rented square for a car is more important than a child learning how to ride a bike in their neighborhood lot. The skaters were the infantry, creating the conditions by which such refutations could be made, creating a power vacuum of sorts that engendered a greater, more democratic use of the space itself. Remote work, the wage economy, and layoffs combined for people to give haircuts in the lot, take meetings, and lead personal fitness workouts; I even saw a small yoga class one time. Everyone had to get it how they were living it, and at the time, we were living tight—space, money, time—and everything felt finite.

While the LARPers were weekly night-owl types, utilizing those pillars with lights in certain parts of the lot, skaters shared space with roller skaters the most. As the pandemic progressed and the world stayed glued to phones, social media helped propel individual outdoor sports that could be shared experiences with others. The floor-wheel predecessor to skateboarding, roller-skating made a prominent comeback. Two popular storefronts off San Pablo Avenue consistently had lines out the door, the demand was so high. In San Francisco, the outdoor skate rink in Golden Gate Park off Sixth Avenue and Fulton was a popular site. The city even closed off John F. Kennedy Drive to cars to allow pedestrians greater access to recreational spaces.

Roller skating was a reminder of how the liberation of recreational space was integral to the civil rights movement. In 1963, Ledger Smith, the "Roller Man," spent ten days roller-skating across half the country to raise awareness for the March on Washington on August 28. FREEDOM, read the sash Smith wore across his chest. He left from the National Association for the Advancement of Colored People's Chicago office on August 17 with a car of NAACP officials escorting him to Washington, D.C. Smith was almost run over by a driver, intentionally, in Fort Wayne, Indiana, and was accosted throughout his journey. He survived.

The New York Times called the middle of 2021 "the summer of roller skates." Though roller-skating may have been a "summer look" for some, the *New York Times* article quotes twenty-year-old Toni Bravo, the creator of a TikTok exploring Black Americans' contributions to roller-skating culture. Bravo notes the discrimination in some roller rinks' practice of "no baggy pants, no small wheels" rules that target styles popular with Black skaters. In the wake of the 2020 killing of George Floyd by police officer Derek Chauvin, there were weeks of demonstrations. Freeways were taken over. Streets were fully occupied at the height of the pandemic, forcing many cities to reconsider the liberatory possibilities of shared public space.

The curbs mirrored the times, with stickers on light poles highlighting the skate history of the spot or conveying inside jokes about the spot itself. My favorite sticker had the word CURBS written in the script of the TV show *Cheers*, but instead of the familiar "Where everybody knows your name" tagline, the sticker's cursive reads, "Where everybody knows your lame." I saw two gents turn themselves into a ladder, one standing on the shoulders of another, to slap up an ANTI-FASCISM IS NOT A CRIME bumper sticker, with the same graphic treatment as the legendary SKATEBOARDING IS NOT A CRIME sticker, plastered high for anyone to see. Writer and artist Adam Abada made SKATE AGAINST ASIAN HATE stickers, encouraging anyone to print them and use them how they saw fit. I made some stickers and posted one on a light pole whose concrete base was my miniature office space whenever I pulled up for a session. I'd leave my little kit of water, a skate tool, a phone tucked into a hoodie. Over the months, more stickers followed, some advocating for transgender rights, others against racism, some just tags on USPS stickers like always. Unity Skateboarding hosted queer skate meetups at the curbs, giving away free product and zines and teaching newcomers who identified as on the spectrum how to push, discover their stance on a board, learn how to slappy on the shorter curbs. The Chub Rollz Fat Skate Sesh crew also turned Rockridge into an inclusive space, a queer- and trans-led community of "Bay Area fat/plus-size skate seshes for all wheels, ages, abilities, genders/orientations." Local crews held skate premieres, projecting their films at dusk onto the white pillars or a makeshift screen made out of a blanket.

Before I learned how to slappy I'd show up and be humbled by the small mystery that is a curb. I did my flatground tricks and did ollies into my grinds—a tell that I couldn't slappy and of the generation I came from. Which was fine here. It's a come-as-you-are space, one of the biggest shared community-regulated spaces in the Bay Area. People bring sheets of ply-wood thick enough to wallride and prop them against the parking block and the supportive pillars, daring anyone to get familiar. Before Caltrans or BART destroyed them, some-one built these fun DIY ledges made of stacked cinder blocks topped with angle iron. Things to ollie or roll into. Slowly I started trying to get into the idea of intentional failure. Sab-otage. Crash test dummies slammed and projected into walls for some greater, eventually safer purpose.

I hated when randoms showed up and left trash after sit-ting around the pillars. Others were more mindful, played good music, and figured out when and where to move their backpacks out of a skater's way as they, too, sat near the pillars or their cars, enjoying what social life any of us could during the worst months of the pandemic.

Watching the community develop at the curbs, I quickly realized how little I talked to other people during the pandemic. No work meant no video interactions. It exposed how little I spoke to folks in general, and how frequently I skated around but didn't lurk at spots like Rockridge. Previous routines of sessioning around downtown, hitting up spots along the way, gave way to just sheer inactivity. Rockridge provided a training ground, a rehab center, a community intersection and model in shared public spaces.

My newfound ability to slappy was a worthwhile change in a pandemic that persisted: combating feelings of hopelessness by intentionally bashing into curbs that led to the accelerated death of my trucks' hangers. When I wasn't staring out at the Bay Bridge framed in my kitchen window, wondering when it would be filled again with the lights of cars, I'd stare at these new marks at night after every session: the diagonal slashes from slappy crooked grinds on my nose and front truck, or the axle nuts holding my wheels grinded and flattened from slamming, instead of popping, into curbs. Looking at my board became a nightly physicalized acknowledgment of trying to face my fears, anxieties, doubts about my future ability to skate and learn new tricks. To survive an unprecedented pandemic by engaging this toy anew.

My unemployment persisted. One day I was so burned by the winter rain cycle that I paid to sit on the vacant BART platform, waiting and watching trains pass me by, the few masked occupants sitting far apart. I listened to a podcast, something news related (couldn't let go), while staring at the sky, hoping for something better and brighter: for full inoculation against the virus, for a time when we wouldn't have to wear masks anymore. I felt my big toe on my left foot throb, smashed and bruised, and debated if it was urgent enough to get an X-ray or if it would heal itself amid this collapse of time and space.

8.

KING SHIT
(OR CAN A KING BE A KING?)

Sun Ra is my favorite skater of all time and I've never seen him skate, nor do I have any evidence that one of the most underrecognized and greatest jazz musicians, performers, and composers of all time was, indeed, a skateboarder—but his heelflips, I imagine, are flicked, lofted, caught, and landed with such immeasurable style that he can only be number one in my heart. Imagine being a teenager, opening up the first skate magazine you've ever purchased, probably in a grocery store checkout line instead of a proper skate shop, and beholding the image unveiled like a secret: a sixtyish-years-old piano destroyer and composer-meets-conductor, wearing a galactic dashiki while executing an impossible heelflip over a car—from flat. How would you react to the feeble attempts at describing this extraterrestrial activity documented in 35 mm, published in a *Thrasher* spread, and presented to you, consumer and new worshiper of this wooden toy?

Sun Ra the persona frequently precedes Sun Ra the musician, bandleader, and cultural dark horse, and it's one reason why the myth of Sun Ra makes him, in my eyes, a skater: an extremely disciplined young man, obsessive about the technical prowess of his craft, who was mentored by elders growing up in Birmingham, Alabama. A bookworm, a library lurker, and a devoted walker, young Ra dedicated himself to mastering the craft and, later, as an adult, sharpening the skill set of his commune-cohabitating ensemble, the Arkestra, which was filled with neophytes and legends alike. But how would we re-act then to Ra leading by example and skating a demo with obstacles so terrible he's forced to levitate on demand over an apparently donated car? Is this beholden image instead a vi-sual vibration, like the approximate measurement of a shadow, an assumed and changing form all the same?

Many of the myths surrounding Ra were popularized by the fictional, trippy 1974 blaxploitation film *Space Is the Place*. We find Sun Ra walking in a forest, adorned in full neo-Egyptian garb, as floating props (aliens?) move through the sky at the behest of his telepathic or telekinetic powers. The film's loose narrative is centered around Ra and his Arkes-tra's music and this weird attempt to get Black people out of Oakland and into their new homeland, space itself. He hums with a gorgeous vibrato a few notes to himself, looking away from the camera, and begins: "The music is different here. The vibrations are different. Not like planet Earth. Planet Earth sounds of guns, anger, frustration. There was no one to talk to on planet Earth who would understand. We set up a colony of Black people here. See what they can do on a planet of their own without any white people there. They could drink in the beauty of this planet. It would affect their vibrations. For the better, of course."

Sun Ra was one of the first jazz artists to seriously ex-periment with electronic keyboards and synthesizers. They allowed Ra's hands to play across the spectrum of the genre that his experiences traverse, from big band swing to jazz standards, through bebop's multiple iterations, to find the Arkestra's sound of the late 1960s and '70s. He created albums that would lay the groundwork for the "free jazz" movement of an avant-garde approach to the form that evolved from the '60s into the '70s. By 1974, when *Space Is the Place* was released, the Arkestra was playing live sets that embodied the entirety of jazz's history in their own unique cosmic bounce, articulating the abstract with newly electrified tools, while also playing the standards and showcasing the skill of the ensemble's dedicated players.

Ra continues, speaking of other universes, different stars, the places illuminated in the titles of his original songs and those few songs with vocals, like "Somebody Else's World." This is Ra's newly electrified period, his Arkestra now beyond otherworldly, taking new sonic "risks," redefining jazz standards, finding new creative heights. Cloaked creatures and extraterrestrial posse members dance in silent solidarity in the background. Sun Ra concludes his opening monologue: "Equation-wise, the first thing to do is to consider time as officially ended." He points his space cane toward the camera, finally turning and recognizing us for the first time, punching the need to officially end time, to flatten it and attempt to contain time by refusing its existence.

The COVID-19 pandemic hits, and between bouts of sleepless nights and constant anxiety I, like the world, recognize the need for outdoor activity, for soundtracks that propel flight. Thankfully my neighborhood holds a space many consider the best place for doing slappy grinds—the act of ramming your board into grinds without ollieing, generally with your front truck bashing first, before the second follows. It's a technique that skaters do or don't have, much like the ability to ride transitions (curved ramps) and do tricks along their coping. But during the pandemic, listening to Sun Ra and his Arkestra's music created within me a new relationship to space, its limits, and its possibilities and the numerous places, bands, and generations of Black American music that Ra helped create and inhabit. It allowed me to crush time in an era of powerlessness and to allow my body to channel music into vibrations, into flight, into skateboarding more frequently, and to learn tricks like heelflips and slappies, those that involve purposely running into objects for joy, to drink in the beauty of such a possibility. Sun Ra is my favorite skater—not because of what he's wearing or his appropriation of space. This is about Black art and Black joy and thus its persecution, its survival against every enemy known to space and mankind—military conscriptions, the Klan, Jim Crow, prudes, jazz snobs, precincts, speakeasies, landlords, cabaret cards.

Our antihero in question was first presented in human, celestial form as Herman "Sonny" Poole Blount of Birmingham, Alabama, who toured from the southern cultural epicenter of Birmingham up the Eastern Seaboard before joining a generation migrating north along the Mississippi up to Chicago, transforming over time into a bandleader and jazz deity—Le Sony'r Ra—and living through the late 1950s on the city's South Side. Civilians and skaters may refer to such elevated alignment of mind, body, and creative practice as "astral projection," but we are mere mortals, trying to describe Ra's heelflips like an on-demand portal to an accessible beyond.

Sun Ra was abducted, taken somewhere close to Saturn's rings, in a realignment presented in the form of a dream, he claims, creating an openness with, and relationship to, physical space that resembles a young skater crammed into a closet turned bedroom, trying to make it in any Urban City, USA. Ra had a formative period of disciplined community education, learning how to read music through intense practice, harnessing his intrinsic skills to sight-read, this tightly wound sonic relationship carried over to academic success in high school. When Ra was announced as his graduating class's valedictorian, he shunned the honor, reluctant to have any spotlight. But that pursuit of the particular, the valued and unseen forces underlying quixotic approaches paralleling life's possibilities, is what Ra's sound informs listeners willing enough to hear. And skaters hear everything—we are attuned to the sonic distance to or from an object, which shouldn't be surprising, given that we ourselves are moving objects, self-propelled rocket ships of civilian propulsion.

At the height of the pandemic, I'd sit on the wood platform dividing my and my neighbor's side doors and stare at the sky above. This landing is my front yard, backyard, break room, conference center, wellness-retreat destination, and, on wildfire nights, charcoal sauna. I'd listen to Ra on my headphones, the now digitally streaming intergalactic tunes, and think about that morning's skate session and what I wanted to try and learn tomorrow, and then I'd wonder if I was sick and breathe in the air, reminding myself that I was outside. And I'd imagine the Arkestra playing these tunes, Ra orchestrating by pointing at different members of the ensemble. I'd carry these sunset dreams into the next skate session, imagining the

Arkestra awaiting me at the curbs, already sweating an hour into this hypothetical, time-bending skate session.

So what spaces would Ra's heelflips inhabit, would these heelflips traverse? Maybe Ra would make a manhole cover rise slowly from the ground with his telekinetic powers, if only to heelflip that much higher over it, new challenges for this mortal's playground. Such interstellar skate demonstrations by Ra would precede a brief poetry sermon regarding physics, discipline, space, time, universes, pharaohs, before he devoted the rest of the evening to music, thus ending the skate demo/experience somewhere in the afterlight of an immeasurable day—and I have to say *somewhere* and not *sometime*, because it is the place that creates space, and space is the place, as Ra has proclaimed many times before. A dance then, with Ra's skating a choreography speaking from a future faraway land, the place from which Ra was abducted in a dream, a place resembling Saturn, according to Ra, before being returned to what his family refers to as "Alabama." Ra decided still to continue his intergalactic journey through the keys, yes, but maybe he also started waxing curbs, slapping the shit out of Birmingham sidewalks en route to rehearsal, landing perfect heelflips between gigs like a double-palm scream of ivory keys.

If kickflips are nimble acts, heelflips are explosions. There is something about heelflips that for me resembles a raised fist—a declaration by those who know the need to squat and get that lift, a bold, generous pop that syncs with a propelled flick. Something about how the front foot of a heelflip can curl its toes around the inside of the board like coiled knuckles, preparing for that kicking motion of the front foot—a flick that becomes a shotgun blast welcoming a heelflip like a gorgeous wail from the speakers of our subconscious—that much weight and cultural gravity when performed with style. What does the back foot do post-levitation, after that pop required for flight? Does it await the flicked board's fully rotated realization, "catching" it for landing? Or does it do this and more, rising still, a new height for the trick, for this raised fist fully extended past the heavens through the hole in the ozone layer, a declaration saying, Right now, right here, I stand and exist and am making the sounds, vibrations, the music that defines my now-flattened time?

I imagine Sun Ra would cast heelflips into interdimensional spaces of liberation where such astonishments properly deserve to be seen, admired, respected across time and space. The memory of Sun Ra performing tricks would illuminate the sky like the gold sequins hand sewn along Ra's and the Arkestra's caps and gowns, so bright any barfly and jive turkey alike would be able to see, admire, respect Ra from across the beyond. He would excel at unique DIY skateparks, ones with enough space to house multiple random objects while serving Ra's need for disciplined, repetitive training. Maybe San Francisco's Flower Shop, West Oakland's Lower Bobs, or the most infamous, Burnside in Portland. Upon arrival, the rest of the locals would quicken their pace, trying to land their tricks before Ra's spontaneous acts reimagine the spot. Beforehand, they'd cooperatively lead exercises with the Arkestra: wide lunges, big leg stretches, and tai chi alignments before warming up with obscenely difficult first tricks—frontside invert on the tallest quarter pipe, or maybe a heelflip into a grind down the hubba ledge—setting the session's tone. Full-cotton quasi onesies, a turban (or three), and a galaxy of shawls tucked and flying around his already-flowing body. No shoes or sandals, just suede huaraches held together with Shoe Goo. I can hear Ra on a proper pay phone asking the team manager to send them boards at the next stop of the tour, boards of specific widths and experimental lengths and wood layers of different-colored veneers to stimulate his energy between tricks, an attempt to capture Ra bearing the weight and possibility of experiencing a pure, self-propelled joy.

————

There's a pedestrian island protecting the bus lane at Market and Seventh Street in downtown San Francisco. The concrete strip has a massive guardrail, at least waist, if not neck, high, dividing pedestrians from cars and offboarding MUNI bus passengers. It's the kind of guardrail skaters only grind with their fingers, figurative daydreams mimicking the superhero hops we wish we had to grind anything that high. Yet months later, a *Thrasher* photo shows Sage Elsesser grinding the hell out of this pedestrian handrail, without any jump ramp assistance, strictly from flat, showcasing the wizardry possible from the power of his pop. On the other side of the pedestrian strip, a gentleman stares at Elsesser's act with my same jaw-dropped wonder. I try to measure if the space between the bottom of Elsesser's board and Market Street could indeed fit the height and width of a car, one of those demolished and well-skated ones from a mid-1990s European skate contest I imagined Sun Ra levitating over.

Pop matters, and Elsesser has it in abundance, one of several reasons that make Elsesser perhaps Sun Ra's closest skateboarding doppelgänger. Elsesser's career took off after the release of Supreme's inaugural full-length skate videos—2014's *cherry* and 2018's *BLESSED*—catapulting the new brands Elsesser and many of Supreme's riders were sponsored by, while also defining Supreme's sponsored team. These films and the brand direction behind them solidified Supreme's new generational relevance in skateboarding as a premiere platform for the freshest, the loudest, the most creative culture shifters—the coolest skaters. Over the course of these projects, we see Elsesser grow up: from the older teenager in his all-black Joy Division–worship phase to a grown man in baggy pants, an occasionally Dipset-purple durag, and maybe a pair of Cons now bearing his name or creative influence, his skateboard deck titular just the same. Elsesser has avoided whatever spotlight the industry produces and instead has pursued a full ride to the Pratt Institute instead of skating—or rather, in addition to skating. This was celebrated in a 2015 Fucking Awesome Skateboards print ad in *Thrasher* featuring Elsesser's dunking board graphic, the text reading "Sage Elsesser Full Scholarship Pratt Institute" opposite an image of the university's emblem.

And music. Elsesser also became Navy Blue. During his recent tours mid-pandemic and post-vaccine, he's asked audience members to begin and end his set with moments of meditation. He's reimagining the audience-performer spaces into spaces of collective awareness and healing. He's producing and rapping and performing and collaborating, modeling between and across all these interests. And I wonder if Elsesser's need to create new relationships with his audience was first achieved through the space he created in his video parts for Supreme.

We hear the keys of Sun Ra welcome us to Elsesser's *BLESSED* part as Elsesser attempts to light a cigarette against the wind. A stripped-down quartet derived from his larger Arkestra joins Ra, featuring his longtime tenor saxophonist John Gilmore. The song is a January 1978 production recorded in Rome entitled "When There Is No Sun" and is one of the few Arkestra tracks to have vocals, the lyrics taken from Ra's poems: "Sky is a sea of darkness / When there is no sun to light the way." Etymological plays on darkness, sun, sky, and time permeate this chant of a song, interrupted by Gilmore's sky-bound solo. It shows a slower, more conventional side of Ra, one outside of his myth's persona but rooted in the skills, his discipline, that propelled his career.

When Elsesser executes heelflips, they are astonishingly explosive, hot-wired with pop. Almost resembling a wave, his back foot tucks into his body to catch the board with his front foot still fully extended—a raised fist still. It's this eye-catching style that's helped propel Elsesser's career, that carves out his own niche in the visual history books of skateboarding through a style that redefines the possibility of a skater's pop. If every skater had this ability, the effect would be commonplace; with Elsesser, the footage reveals something extraordinary, outside a skater's everyday assumptions of their relationship with space. Elsesser's pop pushes skateboarding forward by recognizing and actualizing its possibilities. The song continues, and its strength appears in the solitude, the negative space within the song itself, striding amid whispering brushstrokes across the snare.

Elsesser's part arrives early in the video's timeline, and this part alone creates a new space within a "known" space of a full-length skate video. Skaters press play on new skate videos expecting perfectly landed tricks to be delivered on a platter, at high volume, with the proverbial stoke on full tilt. Elsesser appropriates these skate-video structures to interpolate what he feels is a vision of skateboarding, or his vision of himself on a skateboard, which is to say a documentation of how Elsesser traverses the world.

A key trick from Elsesser's *BLESSED* part demonstrates how Elsesser turns Freedom Plaza in Washington, D.C., into his personal space. Elsesser executes a chest-high frontside tailslide to fakie across the tallest white wall at the spot skaters refer to as Pulaski Park. This trick is so good it could stand alone of its own free will but instead is succeeded by two additional tricks to create a line—a sequence of tricks. Elsesser floats a fakie heelflip on the plaza's smooth tile, his heel perfectly upturned, the sole of his shoe fully exposed, like palms waving in affirmation across the sky to a DJ. The grace and power and the discipline of Elsesser's heelflip barely loses him any speed midline between tricks. He turns himself back to his regular stance to grind, again from flat, a planter sitting on top of the park's trademark dark marble ledges, making the obstacle higher than that first, chest-high ledge that started Elsesser's line.

One of Elsesser's first pro-model board graphics showed him fully extending his arm for a slam dunk on a random playground. The look on his face is part yell, part anticipation, part reclamation, an ascension from civilian grounds to something more. Elsesser's mentor (and boss), pro skater turned brand owner Jason Dill, was correct in an episode of the documentary series *Epicly Later'd* in describing every great pro skater's ability to find their "window"—the height of their creative and performative potential—but when it comes to Elsesser, maybe instead the dimensions Dill was attempting to describe were a throne.

This is how Elsesser discovers his royalty. If space is the place, he has mere minutes to demonstrate his vision of such places and spaces. Therefore, we the viewers are indeed bearing witness to a self-ascension, to a mortal attempting to access the shadows of tomorrow found behind every attempt of every trick. That is both skateboarding and the pursuit of music that Sun Ra hoped would liberate humanity from its own mortality, its own feeble limits. To access something from the beyond was the first step toward self-actualization. What some may call astral projection. Space travel.

———

Jazz, one of Black America's greatest contributions to our cultural fabric, has always found an audience in key progressive moments of skate history through videos. And it's largely due to Blind Skateboards' 1991 skate video *Video Days*. By naming it Blind, pro skater Mark Gonzales, the company's founder, was allegedly giving a middle finger to his previous sponsor, Vision Skateboards.

Gonzales gave Sonic Youth a copy of *Video Days* at the Hollywood Palladium. That singular act, a message in a bottle via random-guy baton pass, led to Spike Jonze becoming a music video director and a feature-film director turned Academy Award winner. What's bothering me is I don't know which Sonic Youth Palladium gig it was at which this momentous event occurred—or if it was even a Sonic Youth gig or just a show the band was attending. And was it even the whole band or just Kim Gordon and Thurston Moore? Regardless, a pivotal delivery for skateboarding and cinematic history was made.

The band watched *Video Days* and were surprised by the way Jonze and other filmers were able to capture skateboarding while they themselves skateboarded alongside the featured riders, crouched low with camera lens turned up, one eye on the road ahead, one eye on the skater, massive camcorder in hand. They called Jonze up to direct a music video for "100%" featuring *Video Days* costar Jason Lee himself.

Video Days is a key reason why tenor saxophonist John Coltrane is the jazz musician most associated with skate culture. His playing soundtracked Gonzales's part in *Video Days*. Jonze selected the Red Garland Trio's "Traneing In," featuring Coltrane and recorded in 1958. Coltrane and Garland were then members of Miles Davis's legendary ensembles, with Coltrane replacing Sonny Rollins and joining Philly Joe Jones on drums and Paul Chambers on bass, and membership later expanding with Cannonball Adderley. Jonze, a photographer for *Transworld Skateboarding* and *Dirt* magazine turned videographer, was simply "trying to capture what it was like being around Mark," he told *The Nine Club* podcast in 2018. Jonze was between the ages of nineteen and twenty-one when he made *Video Days* but knew what he had in his company.

Coltrane's entry into the song and skate part comes just

as Gonzales becomes the Gonz on full tilt. The energy of his skating is apparent in his style, so shockingly smooth and casually fearless, and the streets are more of a dance floor than a course of obstacles. He pumps and grooves through small banks along parking lots or sidewalk cuts, propelling him over hydrants. We watch the Gonz attack previously unskated terrain, doing tricks down handrails and skating both his normal and "switch" stance (opposite foot popping the board, the skill akin to being an ambidextrous pitcher), all while Coltrane responds to Garland's ivory introductory solo with his own, propelling the song forward.

Since *Video Days*, jazz has been used less tastefully in skate videos but used nonetheless, often as a sort of stand-in for Black Sabbath, Led Zeppelin, Misfits, and whatever slew of 1980s hair metal bands found their way into mid-1990s and early 2000s skate videos. Hip-hop and skateboarding coexisted in a crowded Venn diagram including weed heads, rave culture, vinyl-record collectors, sneaker snobs, and those who saw "street culture" as both a functioning and inaccurate definition of themselves and their interests.

Consider Stereo Skateboards' intentionally lo-fi introduction into the skate industry, with its brand identity appropriating the design and aesthetic of early Blue Note jazz album covers: minimalist geometric designs with a brighter palette of colors; a band-like interface with riders identified as sound agents; musicians moonlighting as pro riders to peddle a bigger vision, the ends by which skateboarding is the means.. Stereo's brand identity continues the appropriation that is skateboarding itself, taking a toy and creating something more with the object and its surroundings; this was a toy turned not into an athletic executioner of gnarly tricks but into a compass, a guide through new cities, artists, cultures, terrains to something different, more accessible, and tangible. Killing the idols by asserting oneself as powerful enough to create this thing called skateboarding.

John Coltrane is present in many of these moments, and so are the possibilities of transcendence in one of his peers and mentors, Sun Ra.

When the pandemic hit, my space became a place described as a breakfast nook, this small alcove at the end of our kitchen, near our cat Knuckles's kitty litter and rickety wood stairs that travel two flights down to the trash cans and laundry room. My space became my neighborhood, which included a spot called Space Curbs, a massive wall-size mural at Rockridge station in Oakland.

I traced the first Sun Ra–produced sounds I ever heard, snippets of Ra's compositions sampled by hip-hop producer and jazz drummer Otis Jackson Jr., a.k.a. Madlib. The opening notes of *Madvillainy*, his joint album with master lyricist MF DOOM, are in fact samples of Ra's "Contrast" from the 1971 album *My Brother the Wind, Vol. 2*. The original song is more of an experiment with a new toy, a Minimoog synthesizer, that Ra allegedly recorded at R. A. Moog's Trumansburg, New York, factory, although this is debated by Ra historians. Irwin Chusid, administrator of Sun Ra, LLC, and coproducer of Sun Ra's digital remaster series, notes on the Arkestra's Bandcamp that the sonic output of Ra's experiments with a before-market synthesizer was Ra "exploring the unknown, tapping into the future, levitating thru the cosmic flux, as the titles indicate."

The A-side of the record is what one archivist called "spaced-out barbecue music," including Ra originals "Somebody Else's World" and "Walking on the Moon," both sung by June Tyson. I was entranced by these songs and their chanting, swooning choruses, along with my favorite song, "Pleasant Twilight." The song's second half sounds like a descent, the slow winding pulse of Sun Ra's "intergalactic organ" (a Farfisa) driving forward the heavy chords and respiratory-deprived brass, or resting brass, the masters at work calmed by the touch of Ra's driving intervals, when in reality the song is ascending like Sisyphus starting at the bottom of the mountain, dusting himself off from the rock that yet again is there ready to beat him down the mountain, and I imagine Sisyphus—Hiss to his friends, who know he's tough—wearing a weekday suit, the kind you'd find in Cassavetes's *Shadows* or some like-minded Godard shit or maybe in the photos of Gordon Parks. The imagery of Sun Ra very much precedes the sounds Sun Ra created: How does one find an entry point when the canon says you are mad?

I listened to albums in Ra's oeuvre, diving into his biographies and listening to the jazz standards that he covers, recomposes, and presents to us, the listeners, across many of his albums. I really enjoyed the dusty, lo-fi gem of an album *Bad and Beautiful*. It's a spacious early 1960s recording that sounds like a tape recorder was placed beneath the drummer's ride cymbal. The voyeuristic sound recorded near Hell's Kitchen at the Arkestra's rehearsal space at the time, the Choreographer's Workshop, captures this key moment for Sun Ra and the core of his Arkestra that moved through Chicago's South Side through the 1950s and, by 1961, found a place in New York through a combination of chance, displacement, and work opportunity. It's here that the Arkestra continued its cosmic interpolation first exercised in Chicago amid a downtown scene burgeoning with jazz greats.

The recording combines standards and original Ra compositions, including "Ankh #2," a haunting lull of a last-call stroll through the parts of Manhattan that could be avoided with cab fare. The baritone sax of Pat Patrick is balanced against the light right-hand touch of Ra's piano solo before the deep brass pulls the song back into the city's beyond. I'd close my eyes at night against the pandemic sky, imagining streets, alleys, parts of the city, downtown Oakland boarded up and off-limits to its populace. Close my eyes to lose myself in the space Ra's music engenders.

I spent hours reading the liner notes and behind-the-scenes anecdotes on the Sun Ra Bandcamp page, tracking the new digitizations of previously hard-to-find vinyl recordings. A recording of a New York show from 1977 was released the summer the pandemic started and featured a similarly honed ensemble as the one depicted in the 1980 film *Sun Ra: A Joyful Noise*. On the recording of the set, the group charges through a frenetic set to much praise. Whether it's an old song from his big band days ("King Porter Stomp") or an original Ra composition ("Satellites Are Spinning"), as a listener I feel like I'm holding on to a locomotive careening on and off the tracks, gleefully risking death before returning to form. How do you dance to this level of Arkestra? To this depth of the shadows of tomorrow? John Gilmore later sends us through a new version of "My Favorite Things" that liberates the sound of music itself not from the Alps but from the heights of space. An exploration of new sonic dimensions Ra had been exploring since the 1930s, despite years of economic struggle, threats of displacement, a life on the road.

I am building a safe sonic place for myself, I think, nestled in my apartment's nook, trying to stay sane amid stay-at-home protocols; I am trying to find a space that is my place.

I don't think saxophonist Jackie McLean would've skated, boxed, or played shortstop in stickball growing up in Harlem, casually mentored by local elders Bird and Monk, but I do know that Jackie McLean would rather be rehearsing than be documented, let alone be documented rehearsing. Shot in 1975 and limitedly released in 1979, the documentary *Jackie McLean on Mars* documents McLean's early days at the University of Hartford, where he first taught in the university's Hartt School before creating the university's African American Music Department, established by the time of the film's recording.

McLean's career and contributions to jazz were already unquestionable and decades deep. His prolific recording career stemmed from an effort to fill the economic void left after his cabaret card was revoked during pivotal years in New York. Recording became critical. McLean occasionally performed under pseudonyms on late-night billings. His battles with addiction and drug-related bouts of incarceration still haunt McLean in certain scenes of the film. An affable, bouncing, sober McLean shows a Hartford student a particular scale that, he casually explains, he learned in prison. The Jazz Studies program was posthumously renamed for McLean—the Jackie McLean Institute of Jazz—and still exists today. But on-screen we find McLean tired, restless, still hopeful and fully engaged with his students, but frustrated and fighting—for economic security, more free time to rehearse, and empathy, all in pursuit of that thing, not just music but that big thing called *living*.

This is the life McLean brings to Mars. A life he is asking his students to hear and see. In a class of both white and Black students, McLean reminds the class about a previous assignment to be completed outside of Hartford, Connecticut, or, as the film's title suggests, a region McLean considers "Mars": to attend one of the weekly gigs Sun Ra's Arkestra had in New York. Cigarettes are still being smoked indoors, and as the 1970s continues to electrify and turn further and further away from jazz and toward the boogie and projected glamour of disco, McLean is proselytizing the word on Earth, the beeping blips of the North Star that guided him to this moment in Connecticut through cells, rehab, cold-turkey nights, the beyond, and finding himself again, rusty and present and bellowing.

McLean asks the class if they've done their assignment: listen to Sun Ra.

"It's kind of far-out," one student says, somewhere off camera.

The same student asks, "Why does he have to walk out with capes on?"

McLean's response comes right on the heels of his student's comments.

"He's been wearing those blue capes and playing electronic music since 1957. He's the master of it."

When the student complains not about Ra's music but about Ra walking out in front of the band, "up and down and smiling like he's a king," McLean chimes in.

"He is a king. Can't he be a god and a king? The man's sixty. Been out here starving all these years. Can't he be a god and a king? Man, let him be."

The students pause in silence, low-key shocked by McLean's comment, before some groan, bemoaning his interjections. One student says, "C'mon, Jackie, you're losing us," empathetically but also out of exhaustion.

McLean continues, exploring the dimension of his point with restraint, fervor, and style, like a soloist articulating:

> *[Sun Ra]'s not smiling because he's getting fifty thousand dollars a week to be a hamburger; he's smiling because the music he writes is being played and artistically he is being fulfilled and he puts on a cape and plays his electronic piano and walks up and smiles and lives with his musicians and they have a commune. He's a teacher and a great, great artist, man. And he is not accepted commercially. So he's not smiling because someone's ready to give him a big contract and a worldwide tour; he's smiling because he's a king and he's in heaven—can't somebody smile?*

McLean has to walk the line between professor and artist, hoping not to "lose" the students, before he doubles down, citing his expertise. His students may not like it, but they must let McLean be a king in his kingdom for this brief moment, when the why of his existence as a musician is tested. McLean is channeling every galaxy represented by the four walls of jazz clubs like Slugs' and Two Saints and transmitting that creative energy—and the bitterness of being treated like a disposable court jester—into the classroom, into Hartford, through his instruction. Though McLean's position at the university was, in his words, "stability," it was by definition revolutionary, a coup, or in the minds of some on campus, possibly a failure in the making.

In this scene of McLean's defense of Sun Ra, many are quick to point out the racial dimensions of a white student calling out Ra's demonstrative presentation, which challenges the white student's expectation of what Ra, a Black musician, should deliver as a sonic product for the night versus what Ra, the Alabama-born and big band–trained performer turned solar, non-Earth-defined musician, wanted the white students and the entire audience to experience, let alone hear, during a "set," or a visit from the members of "somebody else's idea of somebody else's world," to quote their song.

And what of the evidence behind McLean's statement that Sun Ra was "starving all these years" circa 1978, twenty-plus years into his newly formed self? Longtime Arkestra member Marshall Allen apparently worked two jobs before an unending Arkestra rehearsal. The Arkestra's matriarch and New York satellite, June Tyson, let the Arkestra stay with her in New York for their more extended residencies: a two-bedroom apartment with Tyson, her two kids, and now twenty Arkestra players sprawled about, the "twenty uncles" that Tyson's kids still describe today, as Arkestra member Danny Thompson told *Bandcamp*. Think about stepping over Coltrane's mentor, and one of the few composers comparable to Monk or Mingus, nodding off in a corner for what few hours of earthling rest he generated in that particular collection of twenty-four gravity-bound hours. And people wonder how and why folks got addicted to those substances, as McLean described, more readily available uptown in the streets of Harlem than anywhere in America, anywhere in Long Island, anywhere near Columbus Circle.

In the case of Black American music and joy, to enforce decorum has always meant to silence, to mute, to restrain, and to put into a pleasant, rationalized, institutional space. And citizens become the first line of decorum's defense via enforcement. What place could Sun Ra find to make the noise he wanted, and what place did Jackie McLean have in Hartford, Connecticut, when it came to teaching jazz, teaching his neighborhood of Harlem, to a bunch of temporary New Englanders paying for the culture to be imported to them, away from the commotion and culture where it was born?

McLean's questioning of his student's response and advocating for Ra's ability to be a king, to be whoever he wanted to be after a lifetime of relative poverty, scraping by as a musician bound to Earth, the third planet, away from the galaxies his sounds inhabit, speaks to the restrictions McLean himself faced as a Black jazz musician in post–World War II New York City. Cabaret cards reigned from 1940 to 1967 and controlled Black art and life across New York nightclubs. An increasingly desegregating, post-wartime America engendered cultural backlashes and scapegoats. A narcotics charge made McLean a victim of the police-backed monopoly that undercut thriving careers, McLean's, Charlie Parker's, and Billie Holiday's included. An NPR documentary showcases a letter from Charlie

Parker—exiled from New York clubs and struggling on the road with lesser musicians and less jazz-friendly crowds—petitioning the New York liquor board to allow him "the right to live" and reinstate his cabaret card. Later, Thelonious Monk details how he was forced to bribe his way through three card revocations.

In his book *Sun Ra's Chicago: Afrofuturism and the City*, William Sites notes that, by the time Ra left Chicago, "African American club ownership no longer represented a new level of Black economic achievement but, rather, an advanced stage of commercial disinvestment—the last stop before foreclosure and abandonment." The Arkestra frequently had to "chase down [club owner] Cadillac Bob for their money." The geography of the city forced Black-owned clubs increasingly south, creating a "lack of an integrated subculture," where few white patrons from the North Side "bohemian districts" came down to clubs like the Crown Propeller or the Kitty Kat Lounge.

I can only imagine the number of racist, bullshit, closed-doors conversations and academic-language hoops McLean had to jump through, grab hold of, and burn down to create the African American Music Department, the subsequent jazz studies degree program, and notably the Artists Collective in 1970 with his wife and several local artists. The program finalizes and makes permanent the assertion and reality that jazz is a Black music, jazz is a classical American music created by Black Americans, by Afro-Americans, and whether we were in Hartford or Harlem or Slugs' downtown or at the Five Spot on the night of the venue's final concert—which McLean played, and the documentary footage shows McLean closing the venue with its final performance—the space is the place, and the place recognizes Black musicians as powerful, skilled, sonic wizards from which we should learn. The power of the institute and the role of the college.

It's visceral watching McLean work across canons—academic and jazz alike—while playing revolutionary Trojan horse from within, building an entirely new department in Connecticut akin to importing a civilization to Mars via Harlem and East Third Street, representing all of these styles of jazz that changed rapidly in a short period, frenetically against the times. According to Sites, Sun Ra had to fight against the unions of Black musicians in Chicago who considered him weird or queer or both, a misalignment with the jazz that sold in the Windy City in the late 1950s, with what made white folks come to the accepted mix clubs like the Savoy, where Sun Ra would play behind a curtain while white female dancers visually astonished the crowd. Think of Sun Ra running upstairs and downstairs orchestrating two bands within a single night, sometimes playing entire fourteen-hour sets just to record himself playing with a band for as long, just to be able to play it back, a free, nearly daylong demo-recording tape of his creation.

What skating and jazz have in common is a disciplined, obsessive need for performative space to truly swing. To learn tricks, to build your own spots, to find new skate spots or jazz-friendly clubs after the previous was demolished. It's this type of persistent stubbornness that skaters might consider good trouble, to paraphrase John Lewis, if it were to link the socioeconomic and racial causes to those of utilizing public and private spaces for a communally produced joy. Jazz was regulated by various committees, including labels, who rarely allowed artists control over their own enterprises. Sun Ra's El Saturn record label is revolutionary in that context, however shoestring and sloppy. Generations of musicians were exploited during this time, and it is hard to tell any story of this time without recognizing this pain. McLean introduces himself in the first minute or so of the film as "an exploited musician," someone screaming from a distant planet to tell his truth about his real home, Harlem, New York, and "what's really happenin'" as he implores his students again and again to hear things differently.

This is why I hate that jazz has turned into this snap-of-the-fingers, cool-cat, daddy-o gentrified stereotype of itself. Jazz is punker than the punks and more spaced out than the boppers will ever know; it's beyond new wave because it's the fucking ocean. Jazz is the first punch against sonic fascism in America short of Little Richard, gospel, blues, the very foundations of American modern music. It's ridiculous to sleep on jazz, or sleep to jazz. It is the new place from which I want my skateboarding to emerge, not from the rage of young distortion pedals but from a discipline that can only be heard in years.

———

Glenn Jones was a Sun Ra fanatic, seeing the Arkestra nearly sixty times over the years, including an early 1974 stint at Two Saints, the new club that used to be the legendary Five Spot. In his essay "I Gave Up My Death for Sun Ra" in the book *Sun Ra: Art on Saturn,* Jones describes the shows as sparsely attended and casual in nature, and Jones never heard the band perform the same set twice:

The highlights of these shows for me were the senses-rendering explorations Ra performed nightly on his electronic keyboards. Often playing two instruments simultaneously, Ra stood with his head back, eyes fixed on something no one else could see, and let loose with a shocking barrage of thick smears, staccato beeps, roars, rumbles, and yelps, at frightening, stomach-roiling, ear-punishing levels. The thunderous agonized beating of the low frequencies of his Moog synthesizer made the entire building quake. It felt like whole galaxies were dying and being born in those excursions.

Such moments took twenty to thirty minutes of mortal time, the Arkestra's sets passing well through last call.

A buyer for the indie distribution part of Rounder Records out of Boston, Jones tracked down Danny Thompson, the Arkestra's baritone saxophonist and owner of the Pharaoh's Den storefront near their Germantown headquarters in Philly. The store is featured in *Sun Ra: A Joyful Noise,* where Thompson, speaking to the camera and indirectly the kids in his store, espouses core tenets of Ra's belief, including the hard idea of discipline, a path to understanding the knowledge necessary for enlightenment. Though, according to Jones's visit, some of the "kids . . . stopped by the store on their way home from school seemingly just to harass the poor guy."

Thompson pointed Jones, the record buyer, to Richard Wilkinson, whose roles included "road manager, film projectionist, records salesman, equipment mover." Wilkinson brought Ra to meet Jones at a Times Square diner. It was foiled when Ra ditched the meeting to watch the newly released *Close Encounters of the Third Kind*. Wilkinson and Jones later found Ra wearing large headphones, "the headphone cord dragging along on the sidewalk behind him . . . eating an orange and nonchalantly tossing bits of peel into the gutter." They pulled into a nearby Burger King to discuss a global distribution deal for El Saturn Records. Jones purchased two hundred copies of every Ra record. He'd meet Thompson at the Boston airport, grab the records in exchange for cash, and Thompson would be on the next flight back to Philly. This was the hand-to-mouth existence of one of the first artist-owned labels in jazz, in the states, in the world.

Jones's accounts of distributing El Saturn's discography are in the book *Sun Ra: Art on Saturn*, which features a collection of Sun Ra record covers hand drawn and customized by members of the Arkestra, before being distributed by Jones and Rounder Records. The cover of *My Brother the Wind, Vol.2*, the album featuring some of my favorite Arkestra songs, is seen in the book in dozens of iterations and colorations, some made with crayons, others with Magic Markers. Some record sleeves were protected with material from shower curtains, each record unique in its physical design, distinct but unified when presented together in the book. El Saturn Records had no catalog system. Each album was songs selected by Ra. No more than a handful of pressings were made at a time. Interspersed with "normal" records made via short-term label contracts, the majority of El Saturn's catalog was DIY.

Back to Burger King: before they spoke about business, Ra spent "the next few delirious hours" talking about how the composer of *Close Encounters of the Third Kind*'s score,

John Williams, "had stolen Sun Ra's music for [the film's] soundtrack," and how much better Black artists were treated overseas.

Jones's experience speaks to what William Sites, author of *Sun Ra's Chicago: Afrofuturism and the City*, calls the "everyday utopianism" that Ra began to embody in 1950s Chicago, then allowing the perspective to permeate throughout his post-bebop-inspired work. Consider the utopianism when in 1958 Ra's business partner Alton Abraham wrote a declaration from Chicago to higher powers in hopes of "better superior power of the living universe to immediately begin to function and work for me."

In a society of postwar optimism mixed with a space race fanning the Cold War, Sites believed everyday utopianism for Sun Ra was "a mode of urban apprehension in which the routine and the extraordinary, habitual life and transfigured existence, are experienced as productively intertwined," where the songwriter and bandleader "endowed his city's streets and trains with a double existence, one that lent shape and substance to the daily lives of community members while also transporting them, at certain musical moments, to somewhere else."

This is exactly how I wanted to feel all the times I skated during the pandemic—that whatever physical energy I exerted through my feet onto these ridiculously waxed curbs would become a new way to escape the present, to embrace something incalculable by economic or employment standards, to do something for the purity of acquiring new knowledge and refilling myself with a necessary joy, one embracing all time, even the hell of our present pandemic. This was my everyday utopianism, I suppose.

Ra's was rooted in a place too—Washington Square Park in the Bronzeville section of Chicago, the heart of the city's African American community, or its "Black Metropolis." This is where a spectrum of new, radical, Afro- and Black-centered (if not Black Nationalist) ideologies converged, and where Ra and Abraham's self-published Thmei broadsheets and pre-Arkestra world views were born. Within this context, Abraham and Ra, "like many Washington Park groups, were striving to create an ethnicity for black Americans through a new religious history and geography of identity." Some were Jewish, some Islamic, others Moorish or African in scope. The idea of nationhood via musicality took the form of club sets that mixed playing traditional jazz standards—rigorously performed and perfected each night—with "exploring and combining two musical geographies—ancient Africa and outer space."

As a composer, Ra accomplished this by appropriating and remixing "the Afro-Caribbean dance music that was increasingly prominent in South Side nightlife culture . . . shaped by the sounds of Africa as heard in Chicago." This was reflected in the Thmei broadsheets, with Ra explaining tactics similar to those he'd explained to Jones at the Burger King: "Taking Ethiopianist philosophical and historical propositions as their starting point, the Thmei texts . . . re-racialize the popular musical culture of America . . . They prepare the way for a still-unsounded music of the future—one that might wake up a slumbering people to its long-hidden destiny." These are the catalysts of awakening that Ra was hinting at.

The Arkestra's rendition of Thelonious Monk's "'Round Midnight," depicted in *Sun Ra: A Joyful Noise*, is such an example. The scene opens to the beginning of tenor saxophonist John Gilmore's solo. In the previous scene, Gilmore, in front of the Arkestra's house in Philadelphia, answers a loaded and somewhat intentionally condescending question from the directors: "How does one of the world's greatest jazz saxophonists stay with Sun Ra?"

Gilmore patiently explains how he met Ra after Gilmore served in the army, the word *discipline* quickly used as a positive term regarding the bandleader. Gilmore joined Ra in the 1950s in Chicago and played with the band until Ra's death nearly forty years later. Gilmore would succeed Ra as the Arkestra's bandleader.

"We had been playing this tune 'Saturn' for months, and I couldn't hear it until one day I heard it. [*laughs*] And I thought, 'My God, this guy's more stretched out than Monk!' His intervals—harmony and intervals—very highly advanced, you know? And I thought, I guess I'll make this the stop."

The film cuts to the Arkestra in full swing, full flight. It's here that we can stare at Ra's hands in frame with Gilmore, his solo taking flight, and you can find the way Ra sneaks in, finding his voice in a unique, abstract, yet complementary play to Gilmore's front-and-center solo. They seem to be diverging, two trains with the same destination redirected onto separate tracks, before finding themselves again, Ra's thunderous chords supporting the end of Gilmore's repetitive two-note bursts. Gilmore's solo ends to applause and praise as Ra takes up the head, the swinging melody of Monk's tune now a type of backyard function meets sermon meets musical séance.

It's one of the most excerpted scenes of the Arkestra's existence because of how the clip demonstrates the Arkestra's true musical, cultural, and historic power: from the abstract to the standards and back again, Sun Ra and his players were masters of a form mortals refer to as "jazz." For them it was a quest, a journey, a discovery of "higher forms of music," to quote Gilmore again; it was a lifelong honing as much as a pursuit, and such momentary examples became even more beautiful to behold after I explored the full scope of Ra's discography during the pandemic.

————

When Ra died, new bandleader John Gilmore told the *Tampa Bay Times*, "The college kids are ready for us right now . . . Whenever the punk rock bands come into town, they go right down to the store and buy our records. A lot of the young groups over in England love us." When Gilmore passed, Marshall Allen took over bandleader duties during some of the group's meager years in the 1990s and early 2000s. A 2005 *New York Times* article ends with Allen being asked for five dollars from a band- and housemate, after describing to reporters how he couldn't afford carfare for his musicians, with touring an economical detriment instead of an opportunity. Allen has continued to tour the Arkestra, finding new support in a digital age of Ra archivists and curators who are making a new audience aware of the world Ra, Gilmore, Allen, and so many more helped create to bring Saturn home to their bandleader.

For many, Sun Ra's 1966 release *The Magic City* is his magnum opus, a composition that is "unreproducible, a tapestry of sound," to quote John Gilmore. Recorded in one take during a rehearsal, the album is both an homage and a testament to Birmingham, Alabama, and the name for the mortal world from which Ra departed. The A-side is a twenty-seven-minute composition, unprecedented before its release. Some ears may have heard an amplified gnat when they put on this record, while many jazz aficionados heard new sounds arriving out of nowhere: crashing honks; a train we can't see; brass squawking itself breathless, out of register, only to find new registers amid the Arkestra's unrelenting play; meters collapsing into waves of howls, all conducted by Ra's hands.

There's an extended version of "The Magic City" that continues the back-and-forth between electric and traditional piano. Like seeing the light from a star, I feel we hear Ra's music late, sounds from thousands of light-years away. And this version makes a big announcement: no fade-out but a final, urgent, explosive scream from all players before Ra flickers his keys away again. Ra is playing what he is receiving from an unknown space, and it sounds like Morse code transcribed into song, stuttering its way along the electronic keys of his right hand and the traditional keys of his left. The end of his song sounds like Ra is crooning, screaming at the sun's escape from the sky, lamenting the day's end in a darkness he illuminates through such sounds, a lantern held to the face of darkness until he has a chance to scream and sing again as soon as tomorrow begins.

It is this space that Ra engenders in me when time and place are so confined, so invaluable, so discussed. As oceans respond to the moon, so too does my willingness increase to try new things on a skateboard in a place like Rockridge, where I can briefly swing through and sing my song for a bit. Learning how to slappy may never reach the enlightened sonic heights of the Arkestra, but it allowed music to speak clearly through me to the unseen forces holding me back, the coiled strands of my molecular makeup that make me forget our bodies are made of stardust and wonder.

It's this beyond, that I discovered through sound and slappies, that creates a new dimension in an already-devoted practice and the space to recognize the possibility we have to create a future that sounds and feels like us.

Can a king be a king?

9.

POETS

I started writing poems around the time I started skating. Probably because skating got me outside. I remember answering people when they asked why or what I was writing, that I was trying to describe the feeling skateboarding gave me. That justification felt corny and aged quickly, so I started writing pained love poems and anti-capitalist stanzas, fifth-tier Rage Against the Machine lyrics at best, but they were something, something "we"—my body, my ego, my growing sense of self and awareness of the forces against it—could work with. Gravity was one force skateboarding made me contend with frequently, and writing confronted me with similar parameters, constraints, realizations that things were hard to describe if their accuracy meant enough to cherish. Similarly, a kickflip becomes a kickflip when visually articulated by a photographer's knowing lens—a lens that is aware of the angles skateboarders appreciate, which resonate with style and the effort to achieve it.

Poets have a ground-level relationship with space. Frank O'Hara wrote *Lunch Poems* while observing and being part of the lunch-hour hustle and bustle of midtown Manhattan,

on break from his gig as a ticket counter and, later, assistant
curator at the Museum of Modern Art. Even with the physical
notes of the prose itself, O'Hara threw caution to the wind.
The New Yorker noted he was "reckless with his poems once
he got them down on paper, jamming them in his pockets or
in random drawers." With a pedestrian point of view driving
his prose toward "exquisite ledgers for the tallying of reality,"
O'Hara described workmen, restaurants, and theaters, with
locations listed in ALL CAPS, with homage. His carelessness
for his own physical writing reminds me of those obsessed, talented, but myopic pro skaters who didn't care to redo a trick if
it was filmed poorly or not filmed at all. The day's vibes and the
knowledge that they did it—and didn't need to publish it—are
such an unassuming braggadocio that infuriates the hardest-
working skaters of the world. O'Hara could write poems at the
bar while painter friends like de Kooning and Pollock drank
and argued. That's the stereotype after all, that all poets are
lurking around, unemployed, in berets, smoking cigarettes to
mark the hours of diatribes around café tables. Consider the
daily documentation done by Stephen Ratcliffe—a Bolinas,
California, resident and poet—of specific, singular views outside his seaside window, describing through repetition across
poems the "sound of waves in channel." Across his epic series
of poems, the naturalism within the prose generates a chanting, daily prayer.

Poets are the literary products of their environments. In
archival photos we find Kerouac, Ginsberg, poet Gregory
Corso with painter Larry Rivers and composer David Amram
downing coffee and cigarettes in a crowded diner booth. Or
we find them in the alleyways of San Francisco's North Beach

next to the bar Vesuvio and City Lights Bookstore, smoking and drinking between reading and writing. Worldwide, several cafés and pubs even have wax effigies dedicated to their writers in situ for perpetuity, like Jorge Luis Borges and Alfonsina Storni (alongside singer Carlos Gardel) at Café Tortoni in Buenos Aires. In college, I'd read my own poems in several noted Beat locales, including Caffe Trieste on the corner of Vallejo and Grant, down the street from City Lights.

I learned spoken word poetry like a skater: I watched and observed makeshift spoken word mixtapes first, before taking my first push at the mic. This was thanks to the debut in 2002 of HBO's *Def Poetry Jam*, produced by Russell Simmons. The show featured Mos Def, parlaying a rap career and burgeoning acting career (notably replacing, in 2001, Don Cheadle in the Broadway premiere of Suzan-Lori Parks's *Topdog/Underdog* at the Public) into a six-season, Phat Farm clothing–adorned hosting gig, with Russell Simmons himself providing an end-of-show sign-off each episode. It was no "Peace, love, soul" à la Don Cornelius, but his attendance was marked present every episode.

I recorded, watched, and replayed my favorite episodes, featuring poets like Queens' Ishle Yi Park, Suheir Hammad, Beau Sia, even Dave Chappelle. And the Bay Area's Rupert Estanislao, a short, fully tattoo-sleeved Filipino punk rocker wearing a shirt of his band Eskapo. His calm demeanor started a love poem called "Empress" that became a growling indictment against colonialism and gender-based violence, showcasing Estanislao's growling vocals familiar in punk venues and on open mic stages. I started figuring out a poet's use and execution of the form, like how Estanislao's body stayed tight

at the beginning, seemingly a ball of wound tension articulating itself at the microphone, before he expanded his arms and
unraveled his stanzas as widely and boldly as his small frame
extended. How the most effective poet's first lines acted as ar-
gumentative ledes, like a journalist's, baiting and engaging the
audience into shutting up and listening without demanding as
much. I tried to remember that the HBO crowds were different
from those at the bars and open mics where these poems were
assumedly honed, places I longed to see as much as skate spots
in Barcelona, New York, Philadelphia. I learned by counter-
example as well, studying those poets who relied too much on
performing rather than writing, but whose performance was
so divine that standing ovations and a bowing Mos Def was all
anyone could ask for in response.

I moved away to Berkeley for college and encountered fliers all around campus that screamed POETRY SLAM in big
recognizable letters, announcing the weekly Berkeley event at
the Starry Plough bar on Shattuck near Ashby BART. The bar
shares a block with the legendary La Peña, a venue and cultural
center that hosted many slams and concerts over the years.

Showing up to my first slams at the Starry Plough felt like
pulling up to a popular skate spot and recognizing all the pros
lurking at their local ledges. Dodge the dart board behind the
bouncer and follow the stools along the bar until a right angle
is made with the kitchen, leading folks toward the back of the
seating area facing the stage. I found a nice, secluded space for
tall folks in the darkness between the sound booth and the
staircases leading to the bathrooms a half floor up. Certain poets with local followings garnered more applause; some even

had audience diehards singing along to key moments of their poems. The interior looked like a big two-story shed converted into an underground arts network's office, with pro-liberation banners from various struggles gracing the walls and the ceiling.

The Starry Plough became a Wednesday-night routine for me, but I found the most footing with Youth Speaks, a San Francisco nonprofit dedicated to literary programs in school and after school throughout the Bay Area. Founded in 1996, the organization used poetry as a gateway drug to the growing trend of hip-hop theater and performing arts pedagogy. It represented a progressive, en-route-to-Obama sort of activism via art practicum, pivoting away from the traditional white male voices of North Beach and toward the teachings of Paulo Freire and the writings of Audre Lorde.

Over its history, Youth Speaks has had several offices, all in San Francisco, but its first office that I remember was a big green two-story warehouse converted into a loft space with an open floor plan. It was on Folsom between Seventeenth and Eighteenth in the Mission District, a short walk from BART. Its nickname was "the box factory" due to its neighbor, a literal box manufacturer. I didn't coin the phrase but came into it and the scene's lexicon from the cool kids, or at least the known kids, whose names preceded them: Chinaka Hodge, Shannon Matesky, Emiliano Bourgois-Chacon. I was roped into Youth Speaks by some of their alumni, whom I met at the UC Berkeley poetry slam series, Cal Slam, and not through one of their signature school visits like these local kids had. They grew up in Oakland and different parts of San Francisco, some even coming from deeper south along the peninsula or getting car rides from parents across the Golden Gate Bridge in Marin County. And they would have not met had it not been for Youth Speaks' free writing workshops. Working artists and writers were hired as poet mentors. They'd take over an English class or school auditorium, leading spoken word writing workshops while introducing spoken word poetry by example: what it looks like, how it's different, why we memorized our poems, and how these poems were not freestyles.

Stepping into Youth Speaks meant stepping into a legacy driven by young people from the Bay. The walls were lined with framed fliers and glossy photos showing the organization's history, including write-ups by the *San Francisco Chronicle* on its annual Teen Poetry Slam Finals. It felt cutting-edge and dynamic, a place with attitude and creativity. First-edition iMacs sat in a row for anyone to use, courtesy of a donation from the Red Hot Chili Peppers. Everyone who worked there looked cool as hell. This was a space to hone the skill and voice I'd been developing my last two years of high school, teaching myself how to write and perform.

From workshop to performance, we followed around many mentors, including Marc Bamuthi Joseph. His workshops were invite-only and sacrosanct literary spaces. A future MacArthur "Genius Grant" recipient, Bamuthi eventually left Youth Speaks to become the artistic director of San Francisco's Yerba Buena Center for the Arts before joining the Kennedy Center in Washington, D.C. Bamuthi would hold workshops at the Youth Speaks office, trying to identify who among us could not only write but push ourselves to find a new performance and writing dimension—those willing to be pushed in any creative, literary direction. We were teenagers, and he made a point to not treat us as equals, in the best way possible. To demonstrate why our voices should be respected as equals', while recognizing we were there to learn from him. I'll never forget one time he literally told us to look at him and "peep game."

We performed everywhere. On BART cars, in MUNI stations, at the bus shelters, and on short bodega walks between. At new public park openings and Caffe Trieste in North Beach. We performed in professional union houses, the big, nice theaters on Van Ness Avenue like the War Memorial Opera House, where the ballet and *The Nutcracker* go down every year, and for the big local poetry slam finals, the Herbst Theater next door, where the United Nations Charter was signed. My writing "career" began by me constantly working on drafts and, thankfully, having other writers with whom to share ideas.

If a poet had a handful of solid, memorized poems, they were offered the opportunity to perform at school visits around Bay Area schools—a small gig but an important one within the organization. It was the proverbial work of a performing artist, creating the audience that will appreciate spoken word by building it themselves.

Finding an unsuspecting spot in the auditorium was key to maximizing the element of surprise. I'd sit there slouched and mouthing the first lines of my poems to myself while trying to remember the final words of the preceding poet's line and my cue to jump up out of nowhere and continue the show with my contribution. We were a live-action poetry relay, passing the baton to one another from different parts of a room. Add the pressure to make our marks and hit those first lines, without pause or fail, to grab a kid's attention and keep them engaged throughout the visit. Stutter that first line and watch a kid's interest fade in seconds.

At Berkeley High School, the assemblies were held in the proper student union, frequently rented for actual bands to tour. Over the years I'd see everyone from Mos Def, the Mars Volta, and Ralph Nader perform on that stage. But as an undergraduate it was me, climbing over the stadium-chair seating, finding my footing on armchairs while attempting to "spit rhymes" or "rip the rap," as so many English teachers not of our culture would attempt to articulate after the performance.

Performing spoken word in schools was the better side of parachuting into a scene, a culture. We were reminding students of the cultures outside these school walls, of the sounds and words hidden in their earbuds between classes, of the forces private, charter, and public schools alike attempt to shroud in the name of children's safety—gun violence, domestic abuse, foreign wars, friends graduating into the military, racism, and police brutality. We said as much as possible because, to quote a friend's student, art was anything you could get away with. This was my life and freelance job as an undergraduate at UC Berkeley, sneaking school-visit gigs for literary nonprofits between classes or on days without class. The goal was to get the kids hyped enough to attend an after-school workshop, poetry slam, or MC rap battle, whatever Youth Speaks had going on; we were the gateway showing them how cool spoken word and poetry was.

The random flash mob approach was inspired by griots. In West African culture, griots are "the narrators of oral traditions," who pass down histories through the spoken word, adding their own histories as they go. We started each assembly with our own interpretation, with each poet performing a few lines of poetry and assigning ourselves an order. We spread out across an auditorium, pre-introductions, announcing ourselves through literal spoken word poetry from different parts of the "venue," which could be anything from a proper indoor theater to a basketball court or a juvenile-detention-center common area. My favorite place to do school visits was Berkeley High School; its theater seating allowed me to walk along the wooden armrests, surprising freshman or sophomore English classes or inspiring older teens and young adults.

We were waiting for someone to validate us—a nonprofit, another more accomplished artist, a foundation with a grant attached, an audience and their applause. Like aspiring amateur skaters who wanted to go pro, we wanted to get coverage through stage time at local open mics and slams, showing up early to get on the list for a coveted guaranteed slot.

I always felt like I was making up for lost time. I kept thinking about how I would've dreamed of having something like Youth Speaks come to my school. The more I read magazines through high school and college, the more Youth Speaks school visits reminded me of how skaters in the 1970s and early '80s were introduced to the possibilities of skateboarding at a school assembly visit from the Pepsi team, skaters like Rodney Mullen, Jake Phelps, Laurie McDonald, and Sylvia Scott. In these demos, skateboarding arrived like a spaceship, the Pepsi team busting out their portable fiberglass miniramp and skating it before a presumably shocked crowd of kids losing their minds at the first sight of a skater's kick turn up and down each wall.

What would I have done in my high school gymnasium if some poet tried to climb through the retractable gymnasium bleachers, grab my graduating class's attention, and speak truth to power? Would I have shouted an affirmation? Or meekly given props to the performer after the show?

The questions are moot, given the performers' intent: for the audience to bear witness to the word.

I competed for and made poetry-slam teams in the youth and collegiate divisions and won nationals on both teams my first year. I was a rookie with credentials navigating a new part of the Bay Area's performing arts scene with all the venues, house parties, new bus lines, emergency cab rides, and carpools making it happen, all while attending Cal.

Making the Bay team meant a free trip to Los Angeles. It was daunting going from a solitary spoken word community of me and my VHS tapes to all these kids. I was having a hard time validating myself. When we got to Los Angeles, I didn't invite my parents to any of the events, even the finals, where we won youth nationals with Saul Williams as host, and where I met him and his daughter Saturn after the show. My parents lived less than thirty minutes away, a short drive in Los Angeles terms, and even visited me in our hotel just outside downtown. Still, I didn't invite them, downplayed the event, and told them that there'd be more slams to attend, though my rookie year would be my zenith as a slam poet.

Stupid the walls we build to define ourselves apart from others, from blood. There was a part of me that assumed they'd disregard my wish and attend unannounced, waving from the balcony—*Surprise!*—and I'd accept this reality from the stage while performing and attempting to remember my lines. I wanted them to read my mind and find my desire for their acceptance, an acceptance of anything I loved that wasn't tied to grades, schools, jobs, success. Despite their many triumphs, mind reading was a skill my parents always told me they didn't have—and that it was on me to find and articulate whatever words were necessary for anything to change.

I remember thinking that I wanted to correct something with poetry, wanted to mitigate the frustration of having to explain skateboarding to my parents, fleeing the house for skate spots, avoiding the security of inside for whatever outside offered, and though poetry wouldn't necessarily lead to getting a ticket from the cops, I felt the need to preserve my voice, isolate it from parental anything. Never mind the families in the Bay who had filled the seats of the Herbst and War Memorial, or how some poets' teachers came out to support them slamming poems about some otherwise-unspoken juvenile activities; I didn't feel ready to talk about it to my parents or any adult in any capacity. I wrote about diseases risking the lives of family members, about a friend's parents who told me I got into Cal solely because of my race, about a shitty experience with health and dental care. I wrote about the reality I was experiencing as an undergrad at Cal and not the growing pains of high school, and still, despite not writing about sex or the drugs I wasn't doing, no invite to the parents a short drive away from the Montalbán Theater in Hollywood where the 2004 Brave New Voices international poetry slam finals were held.

I wish that whatever Hi8 tape holds that final will get archived at some point, some nineteen years later. But at least I have a photo from when I performed at those downtown San Francisco theaters, the Herbst and the War Memorial. It was taken during the big regional final poetry slam, the one where I made the San Francisco Bay Area team. I'm wearing a childhood basketball shirt that reads LA VERNE across the top, the town where I went to school. Not even a Cal shirt or hoodie but an elementary-school-era shirt, like a kid wearing their hometown skate shop's shirt at the out-of-town skatepark. I wanted my parents to be there in San Francisco, in Los Angeles, but couldn't admit these parts of myself that I was nascently exploring; I didn't know if it was right. Skateboarding had magazines with cool guys and sick ads and bold declarations, and writing had none of that until I found spoken word and the writers that fueled organizations like Youth Speaks. If skateboarding challenged the emphasis on organized team sports and coaches, so too did spoken word feel like an alternative, a challenge to the acceptable ideals of poetry.

Paraphrasing Tony Hawk, the Olympics needs skateboarding more than skateboarding needs the Olympics, and likewise it's been spoken word poets who, through the power of their work on the page and beyond, have pushed poetry and letters to new heights in recent years.

After that rookie slam year, I started to help organize the UC Berkeley campus poetry slam, even hosting, wearing a makeshift *Reservoir Dogs* knockoff "suit," a cheap purchase from Salvation Army when it was still on University Avenue. I would become an instructor for Youth Speaks full-time in my early twenties. From Balboa High School in the Excelsior to juvenile detention centers at the edge of the Bay Area near Martinez, I taught spoken word and writing classes all over the Bay, continuing to figure out its pathways, and skate spots, on drives now, doing circles around the Bay to make my classes and workshops, realizing the "working" part of "working artists," thankfully in classrooms and not kitchens, frustrating and challenging all the same.

We even briefly had a mid-2000s tour of college campuses that trickled out through the Great Recession. Universities would reach out for a certain number of poets, and we would fly in like a small group of literary missionaries, spreading the word of spoken word to undergraduates through performances and workshops. We felt like we were part of an advanced talent pool from which new freelance-gig opportunities could be found. When we had a gig in Southern California, I invited my parents to the show at UCLA. My mom yelled out, "That's my baby!" and I nodded, pointed to her, and didn't disagree.

Weekend non-university gigs frequently meant performing at festivals in San Francisco—when the city still had festivals. 888 Brannan wasn't the address for Airbnb but a conference center and venue for the Green Festival, annually hosted by the nonprofit Global Exchange, which highlighted solutions-oriented causes within progressive movements.

The performance stage was in the middle of the concourse. Three sections of white folding chairs divided by two aisles led to a big prop-up stage. That day we had the technological privilege of wireless microphones, so it was only a matter of time until someone decided, without words of course, that they would go "off mic" and enter the crowd.

Folding chairs, by their very name and nature, fold.

Additional weight doesn't help. I decided I would go into the crowd, as the second or third performer of maybe five or six poets. Something to spice things up, change the pace, palate cleanse via disruption.

It was going pretty well, finding my way across those empty white chairs dappling the crowd, lily pads toward our literary performative freedom, trying to land the marks of my lines like some minor-league rapper. I read a poem about a deranged dentistry practice in downtown Berkeley that treated my undergraduate mouth like a science project, shipping poorly fitted fillings to and from its overseas factory and back into my mouth like it was a Pez dispenser living on a layaway diet of imported failures.

By the end of the poem, I didn't die or fall, although I remember someone holding my ankle steady, from necessity or fear, who knows, but the performance worked (that time) and nobody was injured physically by spoken word.

———

One of my favorite gigs was a Power to the Peaceful concert in San Francisco's Golden Gate Park. The musician Michael Franti produced the free festival for a handful of years as a nonviolent joyful protest against the wars in Iraq and Afghanistan. According to a write-up in the local independent newspaper *Fault Lines*, that weekend's festival also marked the one thousandth American soldier killed in the war in Iraq, a number that as of writing neared 4,500.

Franti's band Spearhead performed with the String Cheese Incident. Speakers Amy Goodman, Medea Benjamin, Mario

Africa, Barbara Lubin, "and a host of Youth Speaks! poets kept things flowing between sets." Meilani Clay and I were two of those poets, filling in that turnover period between acts.

I brought a disposable camera and snapped different moments of that hazy, crowded afternoon. Walking backstage with my Youth Speaks contact, I snapped a distant photo of short but popular Green Party presidential candidate Dennis Kucinich delivering a speech between musical acts (much as I was essentially about to do). Backstage I snapped a photo of the two friends and poets who gave me a ride: future *Blindspotting* actor and director Rafael Casal and future data journalist and artist Josh Begley, whose popular visualization of drone attacks, mass prisons, and NFL concussions set newsrooms ablaze. They look like young teenagers here because that's what they are, none of us older than nineteen, Rafael customarily flipping off any camera, in this case, mine. These were the two kids who told me to show up to Youth Speaks slams, to give it a shot, that I could do well. Maybe I felt like we'd made it. Or that I'd proved their point. The waiting periods of performance, when community is found in the commutes, the sound checks, the banal moments that become something more, something greater than its composite parts.

The Gift of Gab from Blackalicious performed next, on the heels of his first solo album, *4th Dimensional Rocketships Going Up* (which I owned). He played my favorite song, "Way of the Light." I got to stand onstage, stage right, while he performed his last few songs, repeating my poem back to myself, again and again, hoping I wouldn't miss a verse.

Thirty thousand people on a San Francisco afternoon look like endless specks of flesh dappled with clouds of smoke emitted from this ocean of humanity, small geysers promising signs of life. I quickly focused on the first few rows and recognized some faces from Cal.

Recently, nearly two decades later, I searched online and found that longtime Bay Area photographer Steve Rhodes documented the festival. A photograph shows me wearing the yellow Modest Mouse shirt I'd bought at their stint at the Fillmore the fall before. My hair was a big mass of curly, unwashed locks. The stage-left clock reads nearly 3:00 p.m. The tule fog is visible through Speedway Meadows.

I performed a poem I'd done dozens of times, in national competitions and cafés across the city, and truly wondered how many in the audience had potentially heard or seen me before, if they'd been at the Herbst when some of us made the team earlier that year. My voice screamed back at me through the stage's row of front monitors. I could hear and see out of the corners of my eyes the next band setting up. My poem was off to a decent start, but a commotion was swelling between stage-crew members as my performance progressed. The crowd was reacting where I wanted them to react, laughing, gasping, and cheering me on at the right moments of the poem. As I inhaled to deliver the last stanzas of the poem, the power went out. A generator had blown.

The performance had to finish, somehow. Walking away wasn't an option. I stepped just to the side of the now-powerless mic stand, in front of one of the monitors, without any prop between me and the crowd. I yelled my last lines to the crowd, trying to scream to the back of the park, anything to keep the moment alive. They were confused but kind, quickly putting everything together. With a fist raised to the sky to mark the end of my time, I walked offstage and felt the applause hit my back. Michael Franti was standing there waiting to introduce the next act. He stood easily over six feet and gave me a hug where the top of my head seemingly hit the middle of his chest. The show had to go on, and it did.

The photo I took with my disposable camera shows me approaching the microphone. The camera was in the middle of my chest. The angle places the Shure mic in center focus, with the colorful specks of humanity hovering behind its shield. When the picture was developed, I was startled by how in focus the microphone appeared, like something I'd been training for, preparing to land my trick in three-minute performances.

Those years taught me something new about space, audience, body, writing, and the Bay Area. And how, despite our desires and imaginations, we humans can read words, images, sounds, cities, even audiences—but not minds.

PURE PHOTOGRAPHIC DOCUMENTASHON
NO DECIETFULL LIES OF THE HIGH
TECH COMPUTER RELM. I SPEAK THE
TRUTH. CAN YOU TAKE IT. ONLY THE
LIER CAN CALL ME THE LIER.

PROGRAMMING
INJECTION

©9 by ed templeton, photo by adam wallacavage

EVEN IF A DROP BEAR FALLS OUT OF A TREE
ONTO YOUR HEAD AND SEVERLY DAMAGES YOU
THERE IS NO CHOICE BUT TO GET UP AND
CONTINUE ON...

Couresty of Ed Templeton and Transworld Skateboarding

10.

PROGRAMMING INJECTION

There are certain pro skaters, musicians, and randoms in your life who offer portals to other dimensions and somehow simultaneously exist in real life. Ed Templeton was one of those portals for me. It wasn't just Templeton the skater, but Templeton the artist, the Fugazi and Dischord Records fanatic, the husband who brought his wife on tour, reflecting the unit, the partnership, they exemplified. Templeton's short-lived column for *Transworld Skateboarding*, Programming Injection, was a key, creative, and encouraging portal within a larger creative portal: skateboarding. An emotionally charged encouragement. Encouragement for something other than a skateboard trick felt rare within skateboarding circa 1996. The storytelling, the articulation of skateboarding's *why* beyond its physical gnar factor, beyond its sports-defined boundary push. It justified me wanting to take photos and bring a camera with the fastest film I could find (or poach) from the Kmart off Foothill Boulevard with the good red curbs out front and skateable loading dock in the back. It's Templeton's definition of skateboarding as an act of documentation—that documentation is intrinsic to the act of skateboarding itself—that opened up a way to articulate the inarticulable things skateboarding creates for skaters who love the culture as much as the act. I was too young for those creative skate writers like Dogtown's C. R. Stecyk in the 1970s or G&S Skateboards' Neil Blender, who interrupted his own late-1980s contest run to step off his board calmly, like a pedestrian strolling to a coffee break, pick up a graffiti can, and spray-paint the nearest wall on the plywood course. Even the ascendance of a young Mark Gonzales as a street skater pioneer in the 1980s and '90s, scrawling poetry in Wite-Out across the tops of his grip tape and drawing his own board graphics, was ahead of my time. Ed Templeton was my portal into the intersection of arts and skateboarding, and his brief column was a compass I used in my exploration of both.

It took two editions of Programming Injection for me to start accurately measuring the lens shift that skateboarding had permitted inside me. IT'S ALL ABOUT DOCUMENTATION begins the September 1997 edition of the column. The title is in the foreground above layers of horizontal crosshatched brushstrokes of off-reds and burnt siennas and pukish greens that blend into the article's background. A tiny napkin sketch of a mullet-adorned skater doing a frontside noseslide down a handrail lurks just above the title, reminding you, dear reader who skates and is probably a kid, that though this is a two-page art spread, you're still reading a skate magazine, in this case the supermarket-news-rack-friendly *Transworld Skateboarding*. Templeton's article features the artwork and skateboarding of Tony Cox, a sponsored skater from Louisville, whose self-portrait—a tilted torso with a long head wearing a striped sweater, head cocked just so toward the overlapped Templeton text—consumes the page and stares back at me from my bed at night.

Templeton's writing was usually found in the margins of ads for his company Toy Machine. Those small-print missives playfully ridiculed young skaters, ads referring to my demographic as "loyal pawns" who "must buy now," the type of faux-shock-jock, As Seen On TV! advertising so popular throughout the televised 1990s we refer to as childhood. His columns were different: "Skateboarding is one of the things in your life, I assume, or you would not be reading this." This prefatory statement undersells the catalytic impression skateboarding made on kids like Templeton—coming from a broken home, nearly failing out of high school while winning world championships in skateboarding, and integrating his artwork into his board graphics like other innovative pro street skaters who rose in relevance and popularity from the late 1980s into the early '90s. Templeton goes on to say that skateboarding is "a lot about documentation," the filming and taking photos required for advertisements and magazine editorials, the responsibilities such demands would require of a pro skater, only to increase in the digital age.

"DOCUMENTATION is important. All the images on this page and in this whole magazine are documentation. Any photograph taken is recording something—a visual moment in time. Any drawing or painting made is a recording of someone's thoughts or feelings." His article notes how people are famous because of the work they did in their life,

citing acclaimed photographer J. Grant Brittain and even the
featured artist, Cox. Because they're skaters. "I strongly rec-
ommend that you take the time to document your life and
thoughts in photographs, drawings and painting, video, and
in writing. Go out and do it—you won't be sorry," he says,
"when you look back at it all, and remember, laugh, cry, tweak,
and yell at the results."

When I started skating, I skated alone for months. The relationship between self, board, and environment was a trinity
I initially left undisturbed. Within this captivity, skate magazines and videos were indeed programming injections, indoc-
trinating me with clues as to what this whole skate thing was
about. But this encouragement, to feel the agency to document
this feeling skateboarding was giving me, was one of the catalysts for even keeping a journal.

In October 1996 Programming Injection: a full-size portrait sketch of a man with a square bald patch neatly cut
from his number-one buzz cut. Above him, Templeton's caption, handwritten and declarative by comparison: EVEN IF
A DROP BEAR FALLS OUT OF A TREE ONTO YOUR
HEAD AND SEVERLY [sic] DAMAGES YOU THERE IS NO
CHOICE BUT TO GET UP AND CONTINUE ON ... We
may not know what a drop bear is, or if such an animal exists,
but we know it caused harm to the head of this sketch of a man
and he survived. The bald patch is indeed growing back, after
all, and the subject stares, unfazed and cool, toward oblivion,
all of us participants in a figure-drawing class of which we are
not aware.

Seeing Templeton's artwork and messaging early on, when

I was learning how to skate and figuring out its cultural nuances, allowed me to find confidence in his passion and vulnerabilities. The artwork and tone of the language was as bold as a punk lyric but delivered with a recognition that our time is finite, which spoke to me. I had a desire to articulate not only what skateboarding was doing to me but the fact that I was doing anything at all. I wasn't inside figuring out how to build motherboards out of bargain parts from Fry's Electronics. In a skate magazine filled with advertisements and projected images of cool, here was someone planting a stake in the ground with their art, asking skaters if they realized that the thing they loved was so fleeting that they had to pursue it. Skateboarding felt consuming, passion inducing, and Templeton's column matched that energy while broadening the scope of its impact.

As I changed, so did the photos on my bedroom wall. Music and skateboarding displaced team sports, visually and entirely, four times over: that early 1990s shift from Bo Knows! stickers stuck on Michael Jordan posters to Nirvana posters I bought at mall stores like Hot Topic and Spencer's Gifts. But when skateboarding and everything a skate mag holds and represents took control beginning in the fall of 1996, the four walls I was privileged to call my own bedroom—something my parents constantly reminded me they never had—began to tell the story of how skateboarding was impacting my life. Each part of skateboarding that I loved had its own section. There was the Atiba Jefferson gallery behind the door, the back of the door adorned with a big promotional poster for Jon Lee Anderson's Che Guevara biography. The gallery was a portfolio of photos taken by Jefferson. There was an Eric Koston–dedicated section on the heels of his winning *Thrasher*'s 1996 Skater of the Year Award, his debut pro-model shoe for éS Footwear, and his amazing part in the Girl Skateboards video *Mouse*. And there was a section for Templeton, filled with Programming Injection columns; weird ads for the brief vegan footwear brand Sheep: zoom-ins of Templeton's forehead with SHEEP UPSIDE THE ED above, somehow aware and quoting a transition-period Snoop Dogg song; and ads saturated with Templeton's signature clashing color palettes and hand-drawn sketches over skate photos. Templeton's skating was literally altered by his artwork; by presenting it to a monthly audience, he created a consistent artistic relationship with us viewers and skaters alike, monthly art doses made by pulling from journal pages and gallery spaces and saying, *Here, you can do this too.*

———

Those who entertained the "here for the photos, not the articles" approach to skate magazines surely missed Programming Injection. But one thing I doubt they missed was seeing Templeton briefly nude. Ed Templeton's bruised balls were the introduction many mid-1990s skaters like myself had to Templeton, through the now-canonical skate video *Welcome to Hell*, produced and released by Toy Machine in 1996, the year I started skating.

We were raised on Templeton's Toy Machine Bloodsucking Skateboard Company—founded in 1993 amid a lull in Templeton's career and the industry at large. Toy Machine's magazine ads looked like scanned pages from Templeton's sketchbook interspersed with skate photos, a punk-zine-meets-first-year-art-school aesthetic. It was *Welcome to Hell* that turned fans into believers, or "loyal pawns" as Toy's ads declared. Templeton's artwork helped open the gates to hell in the handwritten lower third of every ad, Templeton talking shit seemingly through characters from outer planets and maybe even a hell populated by his graphics.

It's in this popular video that Templeton's testicles, overexposed by the video camera's night-light flash, are briefly but fully displayed. After a barrage of barrier-breaking individual parts from the pro and amateur team riders, it's in the unofficially titled fall section, just before the final credits, that Templeton exposes himself and the pitfalls of skating handrails. Templeton's purple and potentially bleeding undercarriage allows the viewer to connect the dots with the preceding clip of him trying and failing to boardslide a rail: his board does not follow and his legs spread perpendicular to the rail. Tempster's carcass is now geometrically positioned for testicular destruction. We see the injury while his penis remains cupped, shrouded by his hands. The camera pans up quickly past the Toy Machine logo on his sweaty chest, a Toy Machine character named the Transmissionator—a Medusa-headed multi-eyed monster that looked so good in enough skaters' eyes it still exists on boards today. We see Templeton's head looking down at the injury and then looking back up, revealing his actual face: the still-young but veteran (even at twenty-four years old) pro skater, artist, and company owner, on camera and bleeding from his sex, wondering whether he has to go to the hospital.

"I've sacked a lot of rails in my life, usually you miss. That was one where I hit the balls and kinda rubbed them, you know?" he rhetorically told *Jenkem* magazine years later. "The actual testicle moved out of the way so the actual skin got scratched and it hurt so bad, you kinda feel like you're gonna barf. I remember feeling like I had to check this out because it felt terrible. It wasn't cut open like I thought."

That clip, an example of the documentation Templeton encouraged in his column, was just one of dozens of slams documented and presented to anyone with this brick of a VHS passport to hell within arm's reach. Shops wouldn't play it when you walked in because kids would just sit and watch the movie and not buy shit. Even members of the Toy Machine team recall doing a nationwide tour of demos, signings, and local premieres of the video just before it went to market—and kids leaving the place completely shook upon viewing the now-canonical film. And I imagine the slam section contributed heavily to such reactions, but maybe it was the priest in full penguin garb at the very end, grabbing filmer Jamie Thomas and pushing him down a stair or two while furiously but quietly mumbling, "You're low-class. You're the tall-tree type." Thomas, one of the most visibly Christian skateboarders of his era, perfectly retorted, "What kind of priest are you, hitting me?"—his tone, understandably, furiously perplexed.

Think of skate videos as a record label presenting its artists' albums in one product. Each skater's individual or sometimes shared part is a portfolio of everything they've done on a board since their previous video part, with skaters' careers defined by their video parts and the most difficult tricks from those parts seen as stills or sequences in magazines. Videos bring those magazines to life, helping to answer questions a photo induces: how fast a skater had to go to clear a certain distance over the gap of a sunken driveway along a San Francisco street, for example. Videos begin with some type of montage for an intro, broadly introducing the team riders, before individual parts take over. Occasionally a friends section of team riders not sponsored by the brand will have cameos of some of their lesser, "throwaway" footage that's just as valuable to us kids, foaming at the mouths for any footage in the late 1990s. Or a tour section featuring the team doing demos at skateparks around the world will interrupt the individual parts, a kind of bonus section or on-site commercial interlude. Some videos have skits, others just raw jokes, or entire sections full of slams of varying degrees of brutality. The best tricks were frequently shown in slow motion for extra emphasis, exalting their glory, while some slams had a similar visual treatment for more macabre intentions.

Timed to the cadence and rhythm of a full AM/FM spectrum of songs, each skate video created a visual story that represented each brand's take on this thing called skateboarding and what it means to their riders. Each skate video offered more clues to the worlds that skateboarding opens. The best part of any video is seeing how each team produces it: whether they send an assemblage of footage to an editor, or if all the skaters gather together, waiting their turn with the filmer, making it easy to track which sessions happened on the same day by matching wardrobes across different spots. These videos ultimately brought high-caliber, industry-approved skateboarding to life and created blueprints from which to learn tricks and style and discover new bands forever associated with those skaters' parts.

Welcome to Hell begins with a full-screen animated devil clawing its way through a screen of blue; the video ends with a real-life religious figure committing what a court of law might consider assault.

Aside from Templeton's testicles, the most discussed slam was slo-mo footage of a friend of the team's crew. He tries to ollie up a brief concrete platform just above a set of stairs. This first ollie is a setup trick for a second, different trick off the platform and over the stairs below. But instead, his first ollie fails; his back truck hangs up on the platform, propelling his body forward, while his board remains immobile at the starting point, or, shall we now truly say, the point of his departure. His hands can't stop his fall and, head- and neck-first, he hits the bottom of the stairs, his body now the wrong side of a right angle. The next image is him, eyes closed, being strapped into a gurney and neck brace by paramedics.

Sitting and watching this in front of the family living room console at the onset of Clinton's second term was shocking, exciting, and terrifying, and it revealed details in a new power, this affirmation of documentation, of framing the scenes in which skateboarding (and life) occurred and were presented. The final fall of the section features Toy Machine's own Jamie Thomas. He tries to use a jump ramp to grind the edge of a makeshift ledge in an equally makeshift skatepark in a parking lot during a demo. His back truck hangs up on the ledge and doesn't grind but instead propels his body to the ground, face-first; a banner for the 1990s band Failure perfectly comes into frame just above the crowd's heads.

For many, *Welcome to Hell* is the greatest skateboard video of all time; for me, it's tied with Girl Skateboards' *Mouse*. *Mouse* was defined by smooth styles, a classic R&B soundtrack, and skaters connecting tricks into "lines" across LA playgrounds. *Welcome to Hell* visualized my worst fears of destroying my body while showcasing the glory of spitting in death's face with every landed trick. It's where David Lee Roth, Kim Gordon, and the Sundays walk into a skate video and help soundtrack an era.

The mid-1980s videos were categorized by the 16 mm and 35 mm cinematic vision of top-down director (and team co-owner) Stacy Peralta's Bones Brigade series, which helped introduce the skate-video format, often forcing narratives and skits that undoubtedly inspired wonder and documented tricks—but whose visual direction wasn't curated by street skaters themselves. It was the camcorder revolution of VHS tape that democratized skate videos with brands like H-Street, World Industries, and New Deal leading the way toward rawer production of increasingly innovative street skating. It proved that skate videos could continue to be straight-to-market, otherwise-bootleg VHS enterprises, where no music rights were secured and everything was guerrilla filmmaking magic.

When I started meeting skaters, one of the first stories I heard was about the *Welcome to Hell* premiere in San Diego. While finalizing the video's titles, the editing software crashed during exporting, leaving Jamie Thomas with nothing to show. Former Toy Machine amateur rider Satva Leung remembered being with Thomas during this crisis moment. "It's bumper-to-bumper traffic. I remember Jamie driving on the shoulder of the freeway passing cars for ten miles all the way to the premiere." All that just to tell his team that he couldn't export the video. That there was nothing to screen. The premiere was off. Welcome to hell.

After contests and before social media and video streaming, skate-video premieres were huge, and still occur to this day, even if the video goes live on YouTube a day later. But in 1996, write-ups would hit magazines with photos of skaters casually hanging out and celebrating under some marquee in San Diego. *Welcome to Hell*'s premiere failure was the public skateboarding equivalent of having your debut album shelved after months of promotion in *Rolling Stone*. Or at least that's how it may have felt to a sixteen-year-old Chad Muska, prodigy of gnar, well poised to become skateboarding's next big thing. But that night—teenage, drunk, furious—he was angry his moment wouldn't come to fruition. He reportedly yelled in Templeton's face, cussing him out in front of an influential crowd of skate-industry peers, many of whom were there to see Muska's debut part in this potential video of the year. Muska was subsequently kicked off the team, his footage removed from the video, and his image scratched off the top edge of the VHS cassette's cardboard box. In front an archway sign welcoming tourists to Weed, California, Muska stood between Thomas and Templeton, arm in arm. When I first borrowed a copy from a friend at school, the VHS box looked like a three-dimensional version of a print Toy Machine ad packaged as a skate video. The stars are listed as the pros along with their roles: Jamie Thomas (editor in chief), Donny Barley (new pro), and Ed Templeton (nothing). DETERMINATION and DOMINATION appeared over a photo of Mike Maldonado doing a massive ollie, sailing through the sky like some heroic skater to and from an unknown destination.

After the intro, Maldonado kicks off the video to Misfits' "London Dungeon." The slow aggro croon eases into the mellow sounds of the Sundays. Fort Myers's own Elissa Steamer enters the frame in baggy pants, Adidas mid-top shell toes, and a TSA Clothing shirt—the coolest shirt and the coolest shoes, a wardrobe she hid for her post-high-school job as a bookseller. She recently described her dual identity in the book *Four Wheels and a Board*. "I used to dress nicely for work; I wore skirts and hose because I was supposed to be presentable. When it was time to skate, I would go to the back room and change into a purple New Deal shirt, baggy pants, and a pair of big, old Airwalks and then go to the contests." The only woman in *Welcome to Hell* and one of the only ones sponsored by a major company in the mid-to-late 1990s, Elissa's part is a standout, tightly edited classic, with her lines executed fast and with style.

Steamer's section gives way to a tour and skatepark montage. The riffs of Van Halen announce SHOWTIME! The footage shows another side of skaters making a living—traveling the states in an Econoline van and doing demos, city to city, evangelizing skateboarding by presenting it straight to market.

Social media IRL. With fireworks, drunk pass-outs, and insane skateboarding across janky skateparks, this section visualizes the titular hell as an exciting suburban buffet, each village filled with skateboarding freaks—just like you.

Like the video's soundtrack, quotes from bystanders are dropped into scenes like random notes excerpted from Unabomber letters. THAT'S MY PROSTHETIC EYE, declares a seemingly unhoused man, very much holding his prosthetic eye, laughing proudly. BREAK YOUR LEG I HOPE GOD MAKES YOU BREAK YOUR LEG GET RUN OVER YOU SON OF A BITCH is said by a pro-church passerby as Satva Leung boardslides a rail in front of a house of worship into a mellow suburban street. Leung has a standout part in *Welcome to Hell*—emphasizing nollies (popping off the nose using your "weak" foot) and executing smoother lines than his stair-hopping peers—and he also bears the brunt of random verbal and sometimes police-sponsored physical violence. First it's by the aforementioned passerby, and later, in the video's friends section—a montage of Toy Machine's peers executing single or handfuls of cameo tricks, soundtracked to Jefferson Airplane—Leung gets the shit kicked out of him by members of the San Francisco Police Department, on camera, to the soundtrack of "Somebody to Love." The footage, shot on the pedestrian bridge above Kearney Street in San Francisco's Chinatown, known to skaters as China Banks, shows a cop throwing haymakers at Leung upon arrival. Leung hits the ground and turns into a ball, shrouding his face. The next scene is Leung and fellow Toy Machine rider Donny Barley, leaning against the China Banks, being lectured by the cops while Leung sits, handcuffed, on the ground. Another rumor

I heard—that Leung had successfully sued SFPD for abuse—turned out to be true, with the skate video footage used as evidence.

The video's finale centers around the two remaining marquee pros, Ed Templeton and Jamie Thomas. The distorted guitars of Lee Ranaldo and Thurston Moore of Sonic Youth help introduce Templeton's part. The title screen reads LOSER KILL HIM WHEN YOU SEE HIM in Templeton's signature, hand-scrawled font. Fashion choices aside, Templeton undeniably rips. He skates fast—you can hear it. Zooming into the kick of the foot for the one-foot lipslide. Grinding the top of a Long Beach fence in all black with white shoes, the shoes lighting up against the magic-hour sun like Tic Tacs across the asphalt. Without the baggy pants, Starter jackets, and backward hats of the cool kids from San Francisco's Embarcadero, Templeton looks like a merch-table kid—in tight undersize skate tees and equally body-molded Dickies—and uptight. His skating proves otherwise. Templeton skates fast, fearlessly executing signature tricks like feeble grinds, across and down every type of handrail possible. As the back truck of the board grinds the rail, the front truck hangs over the top of the handrail on its other side, like the bottom half of a 50-50 grind molded with a frontside boardslide. The risk of feeble grinds is locking up the trick, hanging up on that back truck or leaning too far forward, stopping the momentum, and flinging your body down the set instead. Throughout his video part, Templeton has this sweaty side-parted head of black straight hair, which stays in shape even midair, like on the video's cover, where he looks like Clark Kent's basement-dwelling brother doing a massive ollie at a skatepark under a clear blue sky. In a skateboarding era of baggy denim SilverTab jeans, Templeton skated massive handrails in a roadie's wardrobe, all black with deadstock Vans and their low-tech, single layer of canvas, Templeton doing big rails in them throughout his video all the same.

I love the intentionally kinked and dangerous rails Templeton chose to skate, seemingly dancing on them and doing something different, unique. If you look close, you'll find that Templeton's skating rails without clear, straight exits, intentionally willing danger. These rails extend over gaps or end with kinks, both thicker and skinnier diameters in size, forcing Templeton to adjust and slide longer or pop out of a trick earlier, all while maintaining speed and style. It's here that Templeton grinds the long straight round and chest-high handrail extending out the entrance of Los Angeles City College. He starts with a simple 50-50 before doing an ollie while grinding, turning his body frontside 90 degrees, and landing into a boardslide for the rest of the trick, landing with style and avoiding a nearby newspaper rack bolted to the ground. The song slows from a frenzy into a few sparse lines of verse, where Thurston Moore begins and Kim Gordon follows. Gordon's baselines underscore the song's moody drift to sea, while drummer Steve Shelley's snare drum is either hit so hard or recorded with so much gain that each hit sounds like an interstellar broadcast. From the sweat turning his shirts black or the bloody scrapes on his knees, none of Templeton's tricks looked like they were landed on the first try; everything appeared a battle.

Skaters awarded the triumphant "last part" of a skate video traditionally receive an unofficial crown from their peers, and Thomas's part in *Welcome to Hell* absolutely deserved its placement, from grinding down lengthy handrails and doing massive ollies across and over Goliath sets of stairs, and an Iron Maiden soundtrack precisely edited to the beat and rhythm of Thomas's mayhem. For moments in the song where the riff diversifies, finds a slower, smoother groove, we find Thomas pushing around the corners of an Oceanside sidewalk, in search of the next spot to destroy. *Welcome to Hell* was Thomas's film school and professional incubator, teaching him how to build a team, create a production schedule, film and edit footage to a predominantly Black Sabbath or classic rock aesthetic (he's from Alabama), and center the marketing around all things gnar, blood, death defiance, skulls, and Misfits—not goth but a kind of military-grade jock-core. Thomas's editing excelled in finding the right songs for the right skaters. He employed a follow-cam technique, framing the chest and face of a skater as much as spot and trick allow. Many were East Coast transplants making the trek out west to California in the dreamy pursuit of better weather, spots, and opportunities to get sponsored. Thomas himself lived out of a car upon California arrival.

During this period, Thomas "started discovering the art of skating to music and how much of a difference it can make," he told *Jenkem* magazine in 2016. "Once I got a computer, it was like you can look at every single beat in the music and you can lay out every trick to the beat of the music. I kind of discovered a whole new form of thinking. Before I even filmed the tricks, I would dream up how I would imagine the tricks looking."

Welcome to Hell was a visual blueprint for the life you could lead with friends on a skateboard: do the best skateboarding possible to an extremely cool song (even making a jock Van Halen song cool in my thirteen-year-old eyes), travel the world with your friends, survive the most brutal slams, take pictures, and film as much as possible because "documentation is domination." It didn't show the hangovers, the minimal pay, Templeton's search for a Whole Foods equivalent in Anywhere America to support his already-vegan diet.

But it did show the physical accomplishments and destruction that were possible, Templeton's testicles included. It showed skaters what could happen by stepping into this new world. In the credits, Jamie Thomas does a park-long grind on a waist-high handrail, the footage in slow motion as a Santana instrumental ballad solos through the scrolling text of thank-yous and shout-outs. After Thomas lands his *Guinness Book*–like grind and Santana's guitar continues to wail, scanned still images appear like a photo album. It's here the team appears as a collection of friends, spirits linked and framed in 35 mm fragments proving their journey across the states, hitting the spots seen in this video. *Welcome to Hell* was a warning but ultimately a welcome invitation to skateboarding, or at least to Templeton's freak show that was this foundational era of Toy Machine.

The definition of *hero worship* is "foolish or excessive adulation for an individual"; few terms better describe being a fan of pro skaters as a kid and beyond. Particularly *foolish*.

Praise be the Peter Pan industrial complex generating adult-boys in love with a toy now connected (briefly) to their adult survival.

What happens when you have no choice but to meet your hero? A hero on the brink of being arrested for skateboarding at a skatepark but without a helmet? When the option to avoid them is nowhere in sight and you're a teenage worshiper of this hero's skateboarding abilities, art, non-style style, and beyond, everything by which you are defined circa January 1999?

In the north end of my high school's parking lot, Ed Templeton was leaning against a cop car, looking toward the skatepark, pristine and emancipated by strict enforcement of pad law, while the football stadium loomed behind him. One of the field's former players (probably) was writing Templeton up while I lurked with a classmate from afar. We weren't old enough to fill a slot of the parking lot with a car; even filling the skatepark with our bodies was a stretch, not just because of the crap layout but because of that vulnerable teenage feeling of being seen. I could only imagine how Templeton felt, but I assume this wasn't the first time he'd been in this scenario, his fan base watching him get tickets for doing his job, skateboarding. He's wearing what he wears in skate videos because that's probably all he wears: brown Dickies, a black Toy Machine fists shirt—clenched, tattooed knuckles reading TOY and MACHINE—and a pair of his newly released black vegan-leather Emerica pro shoes, puffy and phat per the times, insane to see worn by their namesake.

Templeton wasn't skating alone. Most of the Toy Machine

team was there with him, skating the park without pads (did they already receive tickets?) and signing autographs, an impromptu skate demo for the youth of Bonita High School and nearby Roynon Elementary. I recognized the Toy team immediately: Mike Maldonado, the "East Coast Powerhouse" who kicks off *Welcome to Hell*; Elissa Steamer, the most popular woman street skater ever; Brian Anderson, a lanky gentle giant soon to be crowned *Thrasher's* Skater of the Year; and Templeton, their coworker, teammate, boss. Small circles of skaters and clueless randoms huddled around the several pros skating the park. The pros handed out stickers from their sponsors and skate magazines and autographed the backs of them. It's hilarious now thinking about a bunch of grown folks handing out stickers for *Big Brother* magazine, a Larry Flynt–owned, skate-dedicated publication, to a bunch of kids, signing their names as proof of delivery.

I was stunned. This was a new, bottom-feeder park that no pro had any business skating, let alone these pros. Cops giving them tickets, tickets meant for locals like us, swarms of kids asking for autographs, free boards, a thousand *How do I get sponsored?* questions squeaking from the mouths of kids like me. But I was mute. Everyone was going skater to skater, trying to get stickers, or whatever else we had on us, signed. My friend nudged me forward through the madness, cluster to cluster, pro to pro. Maldonado was cool about it, not a lot of words but a nice guy. Anderson seemed like a giant, because he is close to six feet six inches, with at least a size-thirteen shoe. He giggled and said "cool" cautiously to every kid pestering him about his tattoos and height.

Steamer was too busy skating, trying a switch noseslide on a big bank to ledge, one of the only good obstacles despite a terrible run-up, forcing her to carve through pointless shallow bowls of quarter pipes to get the speed required for each attempt. I was infinitely jealous of the sick maroon Toy Machine hoodie she was wearing and her perfectly baggy black TSA cargo pants.

Templeton took his ticket and entered the park. Somewhere in my Velcro wallet, I found a yellow business card, waited my turn, and handed it to Templeton. He seemed ... tired? Pensive? In the midst of managing his anxiety? I debated the math of the hundreds, thousands, gazillions of kids around the world who've done the same. I opened my mouth. I said something dumb and honest, like *You're my favorite skater*, or *You changed my perspective on suburbia*, or even more embarrassing, *I started writing because of you*, and a million other words that left him staring at me somewhat stunned and tired. I'm positive my voice broke, quivered, somersaulted in front of him.

But Templeton listened. Processed my life dump as his inner monologue went on a field trip—I just got a ticket after skating all day, am doing an impromptu signing, and now must reckon with this kid baring his soul? The lifetime of a conversational beat passed. He asked if I had something to sign. I handed him my card. He took a longer time than usual signing the autograph. With a Sharpie in one hand and the card against his knee, Ed drew one of his Toy Machine characters, the Transistor Sect—a stumpy cyclops with stick figure arms and legs and a crooked exhaust pipe extending from its head—and signed his name at the bottom. Thanks, he said, and I said the same, I think.

I thought you were gonna cry, my friend said, before asking if I was okay. School was out and we continued to walk where the sprawl would allow—so, McDonald's—our day interrupted by this arrival of the skate industry so close and so far away, me trying to feel yet again that such pedestrian acts made it feel like we lived in a city and not a suburban town, and how I wished we could bring boards to school. I wondered if Templeton and the Toy Machine team showed up to that skatepark looking for a hassle-free session and if we ruined all the fun. I'd keep the drawing with a collection of ticket stubs for shows I was starting to go to, amassing them like evidence of crimes I'd always wanted and recently gotten away with. A nascent, but growing, documentation.

––––––

The year 2001 in the San Gabriel Valley meant killing time at Rhino Records in Claremont's university village. It must've been how I found the small postcard of Templeton's artwork that was actually a flier. The image was a photograph of a kid either spitting or vomiting something out from his mouth, with Templeton's black frames and a heavily saturated yellow background. On the back were details for the opening of an art show called *The Black Sperm of Vengeance* in West Hollywood, taking place days after my seventeenth birthday. The Twin Towers had been attacked and our senior class was wondering who would go to war, college, or neither. I had a car and a girl-friend who had dyed hair, constantly wore a *Clockwork Orange* shirt, was not a virgin (unlike myself), and attended the Nine Inch Nails show on June 6, 2000, the infamously dated and branded "6-6-00."

I was sober, straight edge, and a disciple of the Minor Threat song's adages about sobriety, a supposedly cooler way of justifying this behavior, in my eyes, than the double-pronged honest response that it's about being the child of immigrant parents and the fear of fucking up. I articulated those things too, regardless.

Fucking up meant getting girls pregnant, a DUI, anything to prevent me from getting into a good college, which I knew wouldn't be in Southern California, maybe New York, but thinking about the winter, it was either Berkeley or Davis. But it all started now and here—from GATE classes in elementary school, summer school in junior high, and Advanced Placement and honors classes upon high school arrival. Everything was a return on investments that crossed borders, redlines, race lines, academic tiers for my sister and me to have a shot. Before I quit hoops to skate "full-time," I recalled my parents only really encouraging the full-court pursuit because of the potential of a college scholarship.

My parents were bent on anything related to art or music, and most of my life was trying to prove how skateboarding was in both orbits. Growing up with an all-ages venue within earshot was a godsend. They realized I wasn't "fucking up" as I got older and even gifted me tickets to see the Roots at the House of Blues on the Sunset Strip for my seventeenth birthday. And permission to witness *The Black Sperm of Vengeance* in West Hollywood.

There on the gallery walls were Mike Maldonado and

Elissa Steamer and Brian Anderson but framed and behind glass, with Templeton's paintings overlaid on them, like a Toy Machine ad in a magazine but here in its original, and lusher, form. There was no consistent line or gridded organization for Templeton's work, seemingly hung at will, or sometimes taped to the walls. It made me see the thin line between a gallery space and my bedroom. Hanging documentation of skateboarding on my walls allowed for a distance; to see the captured forms outside of handheld magazines and to have each page torn out from a skate magazine exhibited, presented back to us, the constant viewer and admirer. Maybe this is why skaters view skateboarding as art: because across our boards, walls, school folders, we're curators telling our vision of the culture and to which movements we pledge our allegiance.

Templeton used discarded or erroneously mixed cans of free paint from paint stores, so his bright pastels are all a bit off, nuclearized oranges and hushed pinks and these toxic Gumby greens that catch the eye. Though the eyes Templeton drew in his figures were blacked out and trailing blood, his sketch and line work worshiped Egon Schiele.

I found Templeton hiding with his friend at the end of the hallway before we left and interrupted him with an odd congrats of sorts. Whatever seventeen-year-old me and my friend could muster. How presumptive that in both encounters I felt the need to show Ed Templeton that I was a complete underage stranger totally obsessed with him. I wanted to be his proof of reward for the creative investment process, for any night he labored on the Rubylith paper of a silk screen or over the right color identification for an ad or a board, or for the labor of drawing me that autograph back at the La Verne skatepark. I wanted to be the real-life image of the kid he fictionally envisioned enjoying that extra little something he put into his art, an alumnus of Templeton's skatepark-to-gallery pipeline. I was also doing way too much and had a persistent inability to control any emotion, even joy, without being overcome by anxiety. Maybe this feeling of needing to do something now can only be compared to trying to land a trick, knowing this attempt will be the make, quelling whatever fear preceded the seized opportunity of rolling away.

Templeton was a big-enough name for skate magazines to report on his art in their nascent industry-news sections. In the mid-1990s, Aaron Rose's Alleged Gallery in New York was the first to host Templeton's solo shows. *Transworld Skateboarding*'s Mandatory Information section had a page dedicated to Templeton's *Teenage Smokers* series, a grid collection of Polaroids that took fire after being shown at Alleged Gallery, and a subsequent zine of one thousand copies also published by Alleged. It was Templeton's first proper published work as a visual artist and, in addition to the show, won him Milan's Search for Art Prize that same year, worth fifty thousand dollars. He put a down payment on a house in his hometown: Huntington Beach, Orange County, California.

I don't think most skaters my age cared about Templeton's art, and that's fine. They were talking shit about the other goings-on in his life in the early 2000s, like the rapid exodus of his skate team. After the release of its next video, 1998's *Jump Off a Building*, Toy Machine lost its entire team (sans one amateur) to competitive sponsors in short dissolution order. But at the turn of the century, some folks were paying attention, and skateboarding was finding more gallery and theater spaces. The documentary *Lords of Dogtown* helped to begin the archiving and historicization of skate culture. These self-referential documentaries establishing new historical narratives, let alone the launch of the Skateboarding Hall of Fame in 2009, helped make skateboarding relevant in eyes previously inhospitable to skate culture. According to the Smithsonian's book on skate culture, *Four Wheels and a Board*, "Suddenly, skateboarding was an art, and its memorabilia collectible, worthy of competitive auction prices and museum displays."

Around the time of *Welcome to Hell*'s release, Mike Mills directed a short, seventeen-minute documentary on the Templetons in 1996, entitled *Deformer*. Mills followed Ed and Deanna Templeton living their everyday life around Huntington Beach, much as Templeton documents the world around him. The film showcases Templeton creating the *Teenage Smokers* series, where he questions a series of kids in a quick, flat, somewhat judgmental tone, asking about their parents, whether they're together, what brand of cigarettes the kids smoke. All the kids are minors stealing from their parents' stashes or getting someone older to score packs for them. Templeton's effort seems to be connecting the decaying dots between suburban kids' expected futures, their self-appointed plight, and the profits made therein. Mills plays voyeur, portraying Ed and Deanna's relationship through a milieu of intimate scenes. We see Mills shooting Ed and Deanna from across the street through their open window, with a naked Ed painting an equally nude Deanna.

In 2004, Templeton was one of the prominent members of the Beautiful Losers collective of artists featured in a namesake documentary. Something about the production, or the singularity of the name turned crew, made it seem like a watershed for this collective moment in time, that Templeton was part of something that welcomed him, something that wasn't skateboarding and maybe offered more kindness. The exhibition the collective put on was impactful. The book *Four Wheels and a Board* details how the 2004 debut of the traveling exhibition *Beautiful Losers: Contemporary Art and Street Culture in Cincinnati* "established skateboarding's influence in the art world by including a lost list of photographers, graphic artists, filmmakers, and other artists who proudly claimed roots in skateboarding."

—————

When I bought Ed Templeton's book, also named *Deformer*, in 2009, I felt like an adult. Look at me, on the train, coveting the hardcover corners of this ART BOOK. This is a goddamn ART BOOK that will survive this transbay BART ride from Needles and Pens in the Mission back to my studio apartment in Oakland, which, coincidentally, also makes me feel like an adult, because it's fueled by commerce, money, rent allowing jobs and vice versa, and the transit, zines, and food, let alone ART BOOKS, in between. There's something about a well-lived-in anything associated with a maturity far beyond my cynical reach. A crate could be a couch if you smoked enough pot and found a pillow (or three), but at least I stuck to finding furniture off the street because I was GROWN. Everything is CAPS in this time of my life because we are DOING SHIT in a space in which we live ALONE, voluntarily. It's my way of replicating the stories my mom tells me of spending her paycheck on records in downtown Los Angeles blocks away from her job, spending hours in the listening booths near Pershing Square, this association with work, space, and material gain. And here I was, making an art grant a security deposit to stretch across three apartments and most of my twenties.

Deformer was a comprehensively autobiographical book and a definitive introduction to how a life impacted by skateboarding and punk rock led to the contemporary artist Ed Templeton.

> DEFORMER: *The shaping and reshaping effects of growing up a specimen in the suburban domestic incubator (and the subsequent paradigm shift upon exit) as seen through Edward A. Templeton in the year of 2008 annotated with ephemeral documents of youth, hand-crafted visual accounts and tender fractions of time captured in celluloid rectangles in this ongoing process which only ends with death.*

Deformer broke the isolation of being from the suburbs and not knowing how to articulate it. Even receiving that book in the Bay Area reinforced the significance of whatever was significant about growing up in that gray area between the San

Gabriel Valley and Inland Empire. It visualized everything I was trying to sputter and say to Templeton at the skatepark, about his focus on suburbia, its sprawling underbelly, fervent religiosity, unique subcultures, and searches for joy. He did this through scanned typed letters from his grandparents who raised him after his mother's medical conditions prevented her from properly raising him and his brother, all after their biological father left them for the babysitter, who then abandoned him, having only apparently needed a ride a couple states over. The secret histories of kids just gone from school. Polaroids from different parts of Southern California—Corona, Ball Road in Anaheim, Alabama Street in Huntington Beach, Templeton's home to this day. Iain Borden, author of *Skateboarding and the City: A Complete History*, describes Templeton as "one of skateboarding's most celebrated artists through his close observations of everyday life," with *Deformer* incorporating "photographs and sketches of bodily, sexual, landscape, religious and gun-toting themes from California's 'suburban domestic incubators'. Poignant, messy, and mildly disturbing, it offers frank insights into real teenage life, far removed from the idyllic sun-soaked life typically associated with this state."

It felt different receiving Templeton's artwork as a Northern California resident. As I was growing up, his art confirmed the underbelly of my suburban existence, its odd contradictions and determination to lean conservative. But seeing his work in a different environment validated its reach, its impact. Into adulthood, I allowed Templeton's work to wallpaper my living spaces, a postcard from an exhibit always on the fridge, or a copy of one of the big legal-size magazines for RVCA's Artist Quarterly Project he helped edit that I walked crosstown to the Haight-Ashbury district to snag.

I tried to catch as many of his solo or group shows as possible. Though I didn't relate to all of their work, it was cool performing in spaces where previous Beautiful Losers members like Templeton also held solo or smaller group shows, like the Luggage Store on San Francisco's Market Street, an upstairs wood-floored gallery with big windows overlooking the madness of Civic Center Plaza. I'd host Friday-night poetry open mics for teens there. I was frequently an impromptu host, showing up to support and getting handed a mic instead. It was part of being involved with the local literary nonprofit (and struggling-artist employment-incubator) Youth Speaks. We'd take over the Luggage Store for the night, blasting music in the gallery, setting up chairs in a theater arrangement, but mainly gawking at the staircase covered with graffiti, artwork, and stickers leading from Market Street all the way to the upstairs-gallery floor. I associated the gallery with artists (and surfers) like Margaret Kilgallen, whose storied illustrations of forgotten heroines and handwritten typeface signs that mimicked those downtown and in the Mission District visualized a relationship with place that is still archived and discussed today, nearly two decades after her untimely passing. Folks like Templeton and Barry McGee (a.k.a. Twist) and his beautifully deformed heads and blocked handwritten typeset. However painfully idealistic or bootstrap-driven Templeton, his art, his company, and even the early 1980s Dischord Records bands he helped me discover were, the way in which he lived his life and produced his art allowed me to see that life cannot be lived without trying. Without risking failure.

———

We're approaching the thirtieth anniversary of *Welcome to Hell*'s release and the big-stair and big-handrail era it helped engender. We are also beginning to measure skateboarding's toll on the body, mind, pocket, heart. Much like the rise of the video camcorder and street skating, new forms of first-person storytelling and interviews have led to a greater understanding of the skateboarder's experience.

Skate videos' proven refrain is that carnage is content. I wonder how much slam sections like *Welcome to Hell*'s created a visual precedent or expectation that such "slams" were not just part of the game but survivable, without consequence. Or in another sense—that to become a professional skateboarder meant honorably destroying your body in the process.

The aftermath of a fall outside a demo in Paris is captured in a photo. Templeton is on the ground in shock, eyes to the sky, blood surrounding his forehead and soaking a white T-shirt from fellow pro Kareem Campbell, who is holding Templeton's head. Patrick O'Dell took the photo to document this moment in time. DOCUMENTATION IS DOMINATION said the *Welcome to Hell* VHS box and the spread in Templeton's Programming Injection column—even if it shows us at our most defeated. Templeton's had at least six concussions over his career. Two vertebrae in his neck were his first broken bones at a 2000 contest in Switzerland.

I absolutely hate watching the footage of Ed Templeton

breaking his leg at a demo in 2012. At the conclusion of his *Epicly Later'd* documentary, Templeton rides up a small bump and tries to nosegrind a skatepark flat bar rail. Not a twenty-stair handrail. Not a contest run on a foreign course. It's a trick that the crowd expects him to execute within a handful of tries because he's Ed Templeton. When he falls, Templeton's reaction is immediate—"Broke it! Ambulance!" The filmer's camera goes to the ground. Scrambling ensues. The demo—and Templeton's ability to skate at a high level—is over. Deanna appears crying, hands over mouth, returning to a familiar, sunken place.

Years later, *Epicly Later'd*'s camera is on Deanna in the kitchen she and Ed share in Huntington Beach. The topic of Templeton's retirement comes up and the silence filling the scene precipitates Deanna's response.

"I appreciate everything skateboarding has given him and myself," she says. "I have a bad feeling it's gonna take more than it gave; you've given 110 percent, and I think it's taken out 150 percent." She continues, "Even when he broke his neck, one of his closest friends in skateboarding at the time said he wouldn't be caught dead skating with [Ed] if he showed up with a helmet. I was like, are you kidding me? Are you going to be the one pushing him around in a wheelchair?"

In *Deformer*, there's a photo Templeton took while lying down in a Fountain Valley, California, hospital bed during "#2 of my 6 concussions." He took it from his point of view, his two feet in the center of the frame. His captioned words are drawn over the photo with watercolors or pen. Deanna sits bedside toward his right knee, wiping her right eye while her left is open and staring directly at Templeton. "Deanna wipes her eye of tears—but not of worry—year 1998."

Behind Deanna, horizontal watercolor streaks and canyons of lines spoon together in dark, light, green. She appears underslept but put together, as if they'd come from home and this were a follow-up visit. The first time I saw the photo, one of the most shocking things wasn't the six concussions—it was Templeton wearing a normal pair of Asics or New Balances. That a pro could not appear as a pro all the time. This photo takes up the top half of a page. At the bottom is a photo Templeton took of himself, a selfie with a film camera. He's crying, face red, full of tears, caught between those gasps where feeling, rationality, and body cannot hold back. "Eye to eye with a person cut to the quick—your base self . . . ," his self-portrait caption reads. *Deformer* ends with a dedication from Ed to Deanna, "whose bravery and constant support are the backbone of this project and my life."

Few documented the toll skateboarding can impose on anyone touched by its flames the way Templeton did. It is hard to hear and watch him age before the camera, to have the realization that we are mortal beings foolish enough to follow the things we love while trying to survive. That in the pursuit of our passions those closest to us are affected. Truly one of the Templetons' most lasting impacts is sharing this vulnerability as a couple.

I think back to those Programming Injection columns and wonder about the fork in the road created after a drop bear attacks, the choice to "continue on"—would I have the audacity to ask someone to take a photo, as Templeton allegedly asked a photographer post-injury? Would I tell them not to record?

––––––––

Through multiple iterations of their squad since *Welcome to Hell*, Toy Machine is still considered one of the few industry vanguards, stable enough to hold down a handful of pro riders and have two-page ads in major magazines like *Thrasher* each month. With *Welcome to Hell* sewn into the team's fabric, the current team is lethal in skill level and risk factor, an intersection that has adjusted to the times as Templeton's artwork becomes more digitally polished, but hand drawn at its core, his snarky text powering the brand's print advertisements through nearly three decades of existence. The team's well-received 2019 full-length video was entitled *Programming Injection*, an unspoken homage to Templeton's brief and seemingly forgotten column that changed my perspective on skating and life forever.

I must remind myself of the power of documenting myself and those around me. There is an impulse I acquired from Templeton's work ethic that enables me to overcome the hesitation that comes with the creative process, to leapfrog any what-ifs and dive straight into the labor of trying to articulate the idea, documenting that spark as much as possible.

The goal is domination not over others but over time. Capturing its fleeting nature and interpolating it into creativity. If split seconds can determine a make or a bail on our boards, so too can we achieve something that didn't exist before, through the quiet decisions and actions that lead to documentation.

The act, the decision to try, is the answer, knowing the worst is to not continue.

It's this approach that I inject into my everyday programming, reuniting me with those welcoming flames consuming the ground beneath my feet.

ACKNOWLEDGMENTS

"No Lurk Limit" includes a version of the essay "Open Every Cell: The Carceral Spectre and Sonic Bridges of Kareem Campbell" previously published online in 2020 by *Free Skateboard Magazine*. A version of "Whose Streets?" was published in *The Yale Review*'s spring 2022 issue. Works cited in "King Shit" include *Sun Ra's Chicago: Afrofuturism and the City* by William Sites and *Sun Ra: Art on Saturn* by Irwin Chusid and Chris Reisman, with biographical information sourced from *Space Is the Place* by John Szwed.

A massive thank-you to my editors, Cecilia Flores and Mensah Demary. Thank you, Megan Fishmann and everyone at Soft Skull Press.

Thank you, Hua Hsu, Kyle Beachy, Ted Barrow, Nina Renata Aron, Romeo Guzmán, Cole Nowicki, and Iain Borden, for the blurbs of support.

Thank you, Ed Templeton. Mark Waters. Will Harmon at *Free Skate Mag*. Quartersnacks. The Chrome Ball Incident. Matt Haber, David Ullin, and the crew at *Alta*. Gabe Meline, Alan Chazaro, and everyone at KQED. South El Monte Arts Posse. Liam O'Donoghue. Adriel Luis & Lovely Umayam.

Nappy Nina. Danny Thien Le. Mari & Vanessa, Lauren & Reed, Nate, Molly, Liz, Yalie—miss you all. Camilo Alejandro Sánchez.

My family for their love and perennial support. Thank you and love you, Meghann Farnsworth.

And to the many skaters, photographers, videographers, writers, designers, builders, artists, musicians, and more who make skateboarding a culture—thank you.

© Bobby Gordon

JOSÉ VADI is the author of *Inter State: Essays from California*. An award-winning essayist, poet, playwright, and film producer, his work has been featured by *The Paris Review*, *The Atlantic*, *PBS NewsHour*, *Free Skateboard Magazine*, *Alta*, and *The Yale Review*. He lives and writes in Sacramento, California.